". . . he that prophesieth,
let him prophesy to the understanding of men;
for the Spirit speaketh the truth
and lieth not. Wherefore, it speaketh
of things as they really are,
and of things as they really will be;
wherefore, these things are manifested unto us
plainly, for the salvation of our souls."
(Jacob 4:13)

NEAL A. MAXWELL

THINGS AS THEY REALLY ARE

Deseret Book Company   Salt Lake City, Utah   1980

First printing in paperbound edition, April 1989

Library of Congress Cataloging-in-Publication Data

Maxwell, Neal A.
    Things as they really are.

    Includes index.
    1. Mormons and Mormonism—Doctrinal and
controversial works.   I. Title.
BX8635.2.M38   230'.9'33   78-26077
ISBN 0-87747-730-2 (hardbound ed.)
ISBN 0-87579-206-5 (paperbound ed.)

Printed in the United States of America
10   9   8   7   6   5   4   3

Without forgetting stillborn Rachel, to Colleen's and my grandchildren: Peter, Erik, and Emily, and all those to follow, representatives of a rising generation of destiny who will see things both terrible and wonderful. May they all live so as to build the Church to help fulfill the remaining prophecies that involve the winding-up events before the millennium and that are among the marvelous "things as they really will be."

CONTENTS

CONTENTS

ACKNOWLEDGMENTS

Special gratitude is expressed to Commissioner Jeffrey Holland, Elizabeth Haglund, Lowell Durham, Jr., and Roy Doxey for reviewing the manuscript and making important suggestions for its improvement. I am grateful also to Jeananne Gruwell for coping with my barely legible handwriting, which President Harold B. Lee once described as "unreformed Egyptian."

Appreciation is expressed to William James Mortimer and again, Brother Durham, of Deseret Book for inviting this effort, if not the results. Eleanor Knowles performed her usual but uncommon editing. Professor Robert Matthews' work in his commentary of the Joseph Smith Translation has been a genuine help.

As always, my family is due thanks, too, for some July afternoons and evenings, more of which could have been theirs. Happily, there were July tennis partners who let me do some needed unwinding.

Gratitude is also expressed to those Church members who, from time to time, have encouraged me with specific comments of appreciation for past efforts, reminding me that relatives are not my only readers.

I genuinely appreciate also rare writers like George MacDonald and C. S. Lewis for maximizing the light they received as they used their talent and courage to write so effectively of the stark beauty of the truths they too found. While I do not get my theology from such men, I openly acknowledge the catalytic impact of their writings.

INTRODUCTION

This book is an intense treatment of a vital subject. Unlike portions of the author's previous books that focused on various dimensions of the gospel with discussions of the many insights it provides to us that are essential for coping with reality, this book attempts to probe reality itself—the very center of the gospel plan—the things that matter most, on which everything else hangs, and around which everything else must assemble.

The gospel of the Lord Jesus Christ gives us many truths, exceptional beauties, and innumerable blessings, but at its center are certain truths that reflect a stunning simplicity. There is, to be sure, a certain stark beauty about these reassurances, but one must not make the mistake of believing in them just because they are attractive; they are to be believed in because they are true, and for no other reason.

Tied irrevocably together, these eternal verities—that there really is the living God; there really is the living Church; there really are living prophets; there really are living scriptures; and there really will be a resurrection with a judgment—comprise the very center of reality.

For some, these truths are hard doctrines. They call for hard decisions. Really believed in, they require significant adjustments in one's life, a spartanizing of the soul, for within their simplicity and relentlessness is a compelling urgency that will not go away.

In the chapters to follow, each of these realities receives individual attention. The scriptures have been searched and the extractions shaped so as to underscore them. The illumination from these truths lights up the landscape of this life and what precedes and follows it, showing what would not be fully visible otherwise. We may still choose to look away, but the realities thus disclosed will not go away.

Those of us who are already believers need to make of our discipleship a lean and trim thing, for these times require it. What the living Church must do to fulfill the purposes of the living God will take all that we have, for these are not casual times. Rather, these are times in which there will be culminating events of staggering proportions, so in the midst of such convergence we must pull ourselves together. Jesus' brief stumbling while carrying the cross is a reminder as to how close to the very edge of our strength God stretches us at times.

We'd best know clearly what kind of path it is we are on while traveling the straight and narrow way; it is the only realistic way, the only way leading to happiness here and eternal joy hereafter.

One's response to these great realities is the key test of his capacity. The acknowledgment of them must be made sooner or later. The prompt response to reality is soul-efficient—not in the sense of shoulder-shrugging acceptance, but in getting underway now with what must eventually be. Appreciative affirmation of these central realities is the mark of the astute, while tardy acknowledgment is the response of the naive, the proud, or the wicked.

Without the obedient response to "things as they really are," there are the endless detours and the empty searches for another course of life, a vindication that cannot be realized. Things are as they really are—and not otherwise. A course of life that is wrong now cannot and will not be proven right later on.

At bottom, the search for the vindication of an incorrect view of reality is often the quest for affirmation of our worth or the hunger for preeminence. Our version of vindication is to be lifted up while someone else is put down. God's version is one in which all persons may be lifted up in order to enter into his rest. (Alma 13:29.) In just four plain verses, of which he said "this is my gospel," Jesus Christ defines what is necessary for us to do in order to be "lifted up." (3 Nephi 27:13-16.) Our childish rebelling against those simple requirements will not change them. Our Lord is not a monarch who is afraid of his subjects, and delaying our response to these realities will not make them less demanding.

This introduction would not be complete without stressing that these great, central realities are inseparably connected. This means, among other things, that there are grave difficulties for anyone who tries to cut them asunder, such as testifying of the living God and the living scriptures but hedging concerning the living prophets. Clearly, there are no areas in our lives that are "off limits" to the living God; so it must be also with his living prophets. Even so, in the face of such interconnectedness, ambivalent adherents pretend that it is otherwise.

Lamentably, a few Church members say that they want more relevancy *but fewer* First Presidency pronouncements on issues of current concern. And unfortunately, a few attempt to reshape that which they cannot control, the living Church. By not understanding that it is the true and living Church, they make the mistake of assuming that it is a democracy or just another church. Such a reshaping would be "pleasing unto the carnal mind," for it would suggest that, without the reality of the living Church, there would be no such institutional restraints; people would be "free," like Cain. The church of the living God is the pillar and ground of the truth, as Paul said. (1 Timothy 3:15.)

Unlike those who wander off the straight and narrow path because of indifference, a few will actually defect. Like Lucifer, the first defector, who did not accept the rejection of his bid for ascendancy with parliamentary politeness, these, his minions, will also depart in anger. Like Lucifer, they will take all they can with them.

The Savior's statement about the kingdom's being like a net that "gathered of every kind" (Matthew 13:47) suggests the tragic flopping of some out of the net.

The acceptance of and conformance to these central realities brings true joy; there is a special gladness that goes with the gospel, and appropriate merriment. Yes, there is a mirth that can be heard among mortals who are estranged from the living God and from things as they really are. But it is a melancholy mirth. The jokes by drinkers about drunkenness are but an attempt to mock that which mocks them. Those who boast and chortle about their sexual conquests are boasting of that which has actually conquered them. The backroom laughter of power brokers over the latest triumph is but contempt for those they say they serve; it is also the sound of impotence trying to reassure itself.

The choice is ours as between joyful reality and artificiality with its plastic pleasures. It is a choice that must be made not once, but it must also be reaffirmed every day and even every moment.

CHAPTER ONE

THINGS AS THEY REALLY ARE

Behold, my brethren, he that prophesieth, let him prophesy to the understanding of men; for the Spirit speaketh the truth and lieth not. Wherefore, it speaketh of things as they really are, and of things as they really will be; wherefore, these things are manifested unto us plainly, for the salvation of our souls. But behold, we are not witnesses alone in these things; for God also spake them unto prophets of old. (Jacob 4:13.)

But, behold, the righteous, the saints of the Holy One of Israel, they who have believed in the Holy One of Israel, they who have endured the crosses of the world, and despised the shame of it, they shall inherit the kingdom of God, which was prepared for them from the foundation of the world, and their joy shall be full forever. (2 Nephi 9:18.)

■The adverb *really* is used only twice in all of scripture, and then only for exceptional emphasis. The great poet-prophet Jacob underscored the manner in which the Spirit teaches us the truth "of things as they really are, and of things as they really will be." (Jacob 4:13.)

Jacob's declaration about truth is, of course, consistent with the definition of truth given by the Lord to a later prophet, Joseph Smith: "And truth is knowledge of things as they are, and as they were, and as they are to come." (D&C 93:24.) Thus, while in A.D. 33, Pilate asked Jesus, "What is truth?" and the Savior did not reply, in A.D. 1833 he did reply. (John 18:38.)

The true religionist is actually the ultimate realist, for he has a fully realistic view of man and the universe; he traffics in truths that are culminating and everlasting; he does not focus on facts that fade with changing circumstances or data that dissolve under pressures of time and circumstance. The Lord said, ". . . truth abideth and hath no end." (D&C 88:66.)

The ultimate realist also comes to know real liberty, for "where the Spirit of the Lord is, there is liberty" also. (2 Corinthians 3:17.) When we go against God and things as they really are, as George MacDonald taught, the universe becomes our prison cell.

Where the Spirit of the Lord is, there will be divine tutoring with its emancipating effects. The serious disciple is a really free and informed individual.

What are the special and central and overarching truths that are numbered among "things as they really are"? These and others:

1. There is a true and living God.
2. There is a true and living Church.
3. There are true and living prophets.
4. There are true and living scriptures.

The longitudinality or *livingness* of these incredibly important realities separates them from transitory things, from dying things, from local ideologies, and from other realities that are short-lived and that do not maintain themselves over time.

For instance, in the spring of 1976 there was a Teton Dam in southeastern Idaho, but it is not there now; that "fact" disappeared. On the other hand, in the spring of 1976—yes, even two thousand springs ago—God lived. He lives now. And he will be living two million springs from now!

Much of really living consists of acquiring perspective about everlasting things so that we can successfully manage the transitory factual things, for tactical choices do crowd in upon us all hour by hour. Knowing the facts about a bus schedule, for instance, is helpful, but such facts are clearly not the lasting or emancipating truths Jesus spoke of as being necessary to experience real freedom, for "the truth shall make you free." (John 8:32.) One of the final freedoms is the freedom from sin, which would not be possible unless we knew what God's standards are and kept them in order to be free. The immensely important truth about reality imbedded within Jacob's utterance is accompanied by his instructing us that certain deep truths are to be obtained only through the Spirit of our Heavenly Father. Paul likewise said that "the Spirit searcheth all things, yea, the deep things of God." (1 Corinthians 2:10.)

Oddly enough, disciples are often seen by others as being narrow; they are occasionally taunted for failing to live realistically in the world—and this by those who are themselves intellectually isolated from the deep, eternal perspectives.

But the "deep things of God" are understood only as we come to know about things as they really are. Such knowledge is of inestimable worth. Such knowing is the moral equivalent of the "street savvy" so much needed for the journey along the straight and narrow way. With it, we can have some serenity in the second estate as distinguished from the breathlessness and franticness of hedonism. We will not experience the emptiness of existentialism or the dread of the disbeliever. It is a mistake, by the way, to assume that franticness is really aliveness; otherwise the just beheaded, but flopping, chicken would qualify as being intensely fulfilled.

This planet earth is a mere microdot, we are told, at the edge of a galaxy that is but one of thousands of galaxies. Some urge us to succeed on this particular planet, at all costs, by yielding to transitory worldly ways. Such urgings are poppycock, and a very provincial poppycock at that.

Would we ask someone who is in a jet flying over Europe to adjust to the culture and language of each country whose airspace he is over at the moment? Hardly. Likewise, the disciple of Christ is briefly in but not of this world; it is not his destination, for he follows the living God of the galaxies. The ways of this world are, in fact, alien to the better world he seeks to prepare for. Thus he must be realistic, for to be too quick to adjust to the ways of this world is to be maladjusted for the next. It is so vital to know, therefore, about things as they really are.

What a great blessing for the believer to be able to

see himself, others, and his situation as these *really* are and not as some imagine them or wish them to be. In this sense, as in others, the truths of the gospel, as the Savior said, will really make us free from iniquity and ignorance.

It is vital to know that there *really* is a God, that there *really* is a Savior, Jesus Christ, that there *really* is impending immortality for all men, that there *really* will be a judgment with genuine personal accountability, and that there *really* is purpose in life and a divine plan of happiness for man.

When we know such basic truths as these, then we know what *really* matters, how to approach life and how to view man in the universe. There is great power in perspective. Therefore, the adverb "really," as used by Jacob, is deeply significant.

Our "luggage," as we leave this life, will include the intelligence we have acquired while here. (D&C 130:18-19.) Not everything we have learned will be useful enough to go with us; memorized phone numbers, a brief convenience here, would not be helpful there, but a highly developed capacity to love others will be essential equipment in the celestial kingdom.

The disciple does not disdain facts, for they are useful and helpful. But as noted earlier with the Teton Dam, mankind is flooded with fleeting facts. Paul predicted a time to come in the last days when men would be "ever learning, and never able to come to the knowledge of the truth." (2 Timothy 3:7.) Clearly, Paul did not regard the mere accumulation of information or the stockpiling of statistics as the truth. The truth is a special kind of knowledge—"of things as they really are and of things as they really will be"—which keeps us from being tossed to and fro by mere theories. It is the truth, not just any old fact, that will make us free!

The earth was never flat, but many thought it was, since they did not have the truths of things as they really are. Ancient prophets, such as Enoch and Abraham, knew, centuries before Copernicus, that the

4

earth was not the center of it all. Men may even faint when, as was Moses, they are permitted to see things as they really are, which involves an order of magnitude they "never had supposed" to exist. (Moses 1:10.)

It is noteworthy that President Brigham Young, in this dispensation, said that God knows all things pertaining to this earth, and "He knows all things pertaining to millions of earths like this one." (JD 11:41.) President Joseph Fielding Smith said, "We have brothers and sisters on other earths. They look like us because they, too, are the children of God and were created in his image. . . ." (*Doctrines of Salvation* [Bookcraft, 1954], 1:62.) How emancipating it is to know the truth of things as they really are!

With true perspective comes a sense of proportion about life. Proportion would help us with our priorities. For instance, clearly one would not forgo partaking of the sacrament because he is trying to lose weight, yet some neglect the scriptures because they are too busy minding the cares of the world.

Today's scholars smile at the friends of Galileo who refused to look through his telescope because they did not wish to see things as they really are. But we too are so provincial when v.e speak of outer space. Outer from whom? Not from God! Outer from what? God has told us there is "no space in the which there is no kingdom." (D&C 88:37.)

In our provincialism, we are sometimes like boys at play in a backyard who, in order to feel manly, imagine themselves to be alone in a wilderness, or, huddled in a tree house, think themselves to be on a lonely peak in the Himalayas. Many adults, in the midst of our unappreciated and unacknowledged divine blessings, are like the fishes swimming in a bowl: heedless of who changes the water and who puts in the food pellets. The precise tilt of this planet that gives us livable temperatures on so much of the earth's surface is but one of our many unacknowledged blessings for which we do not thank God each night, though well we might.

Nor do we sufficiently acknowledge the instinctive things within us that permit us to achieve, for we do not give credit for the divine placement of those instincts within us. Little birds each spring teeter briefly on the edges of their nests and, without seemingly understanding the laws of aerodynamics, they first flutter and then soar.

Having a basic sense of direction about life makes all the difference, because if we don't understand things as they really are, then we may wrongly conclude that man is alone in the universe without the redeeming and living God. Such a mistakenly narrow view can cause people either to despair, which is wrong, or to have an inflated sense of self-sufficiency, which is equally wrong and perhaps more dangerous.

When we understand things as they *really* are, we will understand that each of our lives is actually lived out in an astral amphitheatre where, as Paul said, we are "compassed about with so great a cloud of witnesses." (Hebrews 12:1.) There is never any really private behavior, so there can really be no private morality. And when we mortals are lonely, it is not a loneliness that mortal crowds can cure. We could be in a filled Olympic stadium and still miss Him and home!

The author remembers seeing a child take a piece of toast his mother had told him not to take from the breakfast table, and eating it with his eyes closed tightly. His mother asked him why his eyes were tightly closed, and he said, "So you won't see me eating the toast!" Children are not alone in such pretending about being alone and unseen.

Knowing how things really are permits us not only to utilize those truths of overarching significance, but also to test all mortal propositions thereby, lest we be victimized by fleeting time with its tempting tradeoffs. It is so easy to make the error of Esau, if we lose our perspective under pressure. It is so easy to try to cling to things that will dissolve anyway, in a decade or sooner. The fine young man who had lived well, but who, Jesus said, lacked one thing, could not bring himself to sell all that he had and to give to the poor; he traded a chance for discipleship for an inventory of perishables.

Time makes of the praise and honors of men so much cotton candy—it is sweet, but melts in one's mouth quickly. Yet how many have paid such a terrible price for that transitory taste. The problem with approaching life on the basis of "now" is that "now" is over, even as one says the very word.

If we do not cling to these eternal realities, time can be used to manipulate us, especially by Lucifer, the great exponent of "now." He is also deft at manipulating us mortals by pushing one desire against another, like so many tumbling dominoes. He can use one man's desire for business profits to feed another man's alcoholism; a woman's immodest dress to kindle lust in another man's shaky marriage. Evil has its own ecology, its own interlocking arrangement of appetites. Hence it is so easy to get caught in the webbing of the world.

Instead, for instance, of having men understand who they really are and why they are really here on this planet, the adversary will try to persuade all those whom he can that sin is either permissible or inevitable. Only if we give place for the gospel in our lives can we avoid giving up as the adversary advocates.

Satan is very apt at using any momentum he has in order to make it look as though he has already prevailed. No wonder obvious exceptions irritate him so! Though he postures as a nonconformist, my, how the adversary likes his lemmings to line up and march—toward self-destruction—to the most conforming cadence caller of them all!

In the classic confrontation with Korihor, the agnostic, both Satan and his arguments finally collapsed. He admitted that he taught certain falsehoods because they were "pleasing unto the carnal mind." (Alma 30:53.) Korihor also said, by playing to the galleries, that he received so much reinforcement that he finally deceived himself. He was neither the first nor the last individual to be taken in by himself while being cheered on by a manipulated majority.

The truths of the gospel, or things as they really are, confront not just the Korihors, but all of us. The lazy individual meets, head on, truths about the essentialness of work. The selfish and idle rich meet, head on, the truths about our need to share: they must also ponder the need to accept, one day, the law of consecration. The selfish and idle poor collide with the harsh truths about covetousness and envy. The salacious must come to grips with the truths about the need to avoid both actual and mental sexual immorality. The "eat, drink, and be merry" crowd is confronted with the truths about personal accountability and the inevitable judgment.

Those who are addicted to the honors and praise of the world meet up with the gospel truths about how hearts so set upon the things of the world must be broken. Ungrateful children bump into the truths about their obligations to parents. Abortionists meet the truths about our individual identity as spirits *and* the nearness of the imposing sixth commandment.

None of these confrontive truths is "pleasing unto the carnal mind." Instead, each is jarring, disconcerting, and irritating to the carnal mind.

The prophet Moroni said, "Despair cometh because of iniquity." (Moroni 10:22.) When iniquity increases, so do despair and alienation. Paul also said the ignorance of the everlasting truths would cause unbelievers to be "alienated from the life of God." (Ephesians 4:18.) No wonder we despair when we sin, because we act against our own interests and against who we really are. When we are imprisoned by iniquity, we turn the cell lock ourselves.

It is striking when one catalogs those virtues that come to the fore when people act from an eternal perspective and then also catalogs those virtues that are necessary for wise mortal civilization. What does one see? He sees in both the urgent need for brotherhood and civility. He sees in gospel goals the requirement for self-discipline—and then the same requirement for a free society, since a republic rests, as an unknown writer has said, on "obedience to the unenforceable"; people must checkreign their appetites for their own good and for the good of society.

He sees, both in the celestial culture for which he is preparing and in our civilization which he struggles to maintain, that a high premium is placed on individual accountability. He sees in both settings the importance of deferred gratification so that the emphasis on *now* does not swallow up everything else; there must be thought and deference to generations yet unborn. He sees in both the requirements for real regard for the basic institution of the family.

Both the man of religion and the civilized man see the need to avoid covetousness, for envy is still envy even when it is politicized. Both also see the importance of not bearing false witness either by gossip or by inaccurate and misleading headlines.

In both a theocracy and a genuine democracy there is an overriding concern with personal freedom, for neither personal nor political liberty will last long when inappropriate appetites go unchecked in displays of disregard for people and their property. Salvation and secular survival require the same virtues in the citizenry. The plea for basic values is also a fervent plea for the preservation of civilization, which values must accord with things as they really are.

No wonder we need timeless truths against which to test the lures of the moment. The great truths about things as they really are are immune to obsolescence.

The trueness of immortal things sets them apart from the falseness (or the only partial verity) of many other things. But many people run from these as from other realities. "The masses feel that it is easy to flee from reality, when it is the most difficult thing in the world." (Ortega Y. Gassett.)

For the partial believer or the unbeliever these basic

truths are audacious assertions. Audacity does not guarantee accuracy, of course, but neither are directness and simplicity reasons *per se* for rejecting something.

The word *reality* actually appears only once in all of scripture. Jacob employs the word to plead with his readers to awaken to reality, including the truth that "the way for man is narrow, but it lieth in a straight course before him." At the end of that straight course is a gate where Jesus, the Holy One of Israel, is the gate-keeper "and he employeth no servant there; and there is none other way." Jacob then stresses that Jesus will not open the gate to any who refuse to "consider them-selves fools before God, and come down in the depths of humility." (2 Nephi 9:41-42, 47.) But the foolishness spoken of is a prelude to real knowledge.

Alma describes the growth of faith and how faith can actually become knowledge with the accompanying intellectual and emotional experiences of the believer. After the understanding of the believer has been enlarged and his mind has been expanded, Alma asks, "O then, is not this real?" It is real, he says, because it is "discernible, therefore ye must know that it is good." (Alma 32:35.)

The truth of each divine doctrine is actually discernible by us in a system of certification and confirmation that justifies our saying, "I know!"

This precious perspective about reality that came from God through his prophets surely tells us about "things as they really are and things as they really will be"; it is the only kind of perspective that can rescue us from the myopic mortal view we have about the relative importance of things. This was laid bare by C. S. Lewis:

"We are half-hearted creatures, fooling about with drink and sex and ambition when infinite joy is offered us, like an ignorant child who wants to go on making mud pies in the slum because he cannot imagine what is meant by an offer of a holiday at the sea. . . . We are far too easily pleased." (*A Mind Awake*, p. 168.)

Those who stoutly deny the existence of ordering

principles in the universe, nevertheless, certify in their manner of living a keen sense of some realities.*

Coming to see things as they really are will, of course, make one a member of a minority, a sometimes despised minority at that. The dozen or so scriptures that bear directly upon discipleship sometimes describe such followers as bearing the crosses and the shame of the world. (2 Nephi 9:18.) Jacob describes how he had to suffer his cross and "bear the shame of the world" (Jacob 1:8), suggesting that the burden of the true believer is that not only his behavior but also his beliefs about reality will cause him to be viewed with disdain (and perhaps even contempt) by some of the people of the world.

Coming to see things as they really are involves action as well as contemplation. In various places, the Savior and his prophets speak of taking up one's cross by, specifically, praying vocally before the world as well as in secret, denoting the openness that is part of the Christian's religious commitments. (D&C 23:6.) Elsewhere we read: Take up your cross and follow me and keep my commandments. (D&C 56:2.) Then, if we are to take up our cross and follow the Savior, we are to feed his sheep, stressing the duties we have as disciples to care for other members of the flock. (D&C 112:14.) In yet another place, we are told to take up our cross and forsake our sensuality and deny ourselves such unworthy thoughts. (3 Nephi 12:29-30.) We are to deny ourselves other things, too. In another utterance, Jesus suggested we take up our cross *daily*, suggesting the regularity of the commitment rather than seeing the shouldering as something that can be done in one ringing declaration. (Luke 9:23.) This taking up will also finally require us to give up and do the one thing we lack, whatsoever hard thing this may be for us, indi-

---

*Professors of philosophy often discuss the reality of reality, sometimes with great intensity and sometimes with bemused detachment—but they always cash their paychecks.

vidually, such as selling all and giving to the poor. (Mark 10:21.)

Thus the taking up of the cross suggests a series of specific duties that, if pursued, will put us at variance with much of the world.

We could scarcely endure the crosses of the world without knowing the truth of things as they really are.

The act of crucifixion was considered a shameful thing to have to endure, exquisitely so for a totally innocent Jesus. For us as disciples to be in full view of others (some of whom will regard our discipleship as *prima facie* evidence of our ignorance or naivete) can produce a situation of scorn or shame.

How are we to react to such reactions? To *despise* the shame of the world or a cross of the world does not suggest contempt for others who live differently, because a true disciple is one who has a highly developed love of God and all men. Nor would such despising suggest a disdain for life, which is such a great gift from God. Rather, despising the shame of the world suggests to look down upon such an errant evaluation of us, just as Jesus did. Paul said in Hebrews that Jesus "endured the cross, despising the shame" of it all. (Hebrews 12:2.)

We tend to think of the word *despise* as being synonymous with hate rather than as an attitude in which something is regarded as of negligible importance. Moreover, to despise also means to hold oneself above that which is unworthy. Nevertheless, those who are looked down upon by the world manage to hold themselves above all of that. We must endure the contempt of others without reciprocating that contempt. (See Jacob 4:3.)

Knowing the truth of things as they really will be helps immensely in meeting this challenge; indeed, it is essential.

Paul describes the enemies of the cross of Christ as being those individuals whose God is "their belly" and who mind earthly things. (Romans 16:18.) Some people revel in the unrighteous life but still hold those who lead the righteous life in contempt and shame. President Joseph F. Smith said that a people so set apart are sometimes easy to set upon; "I do not believe there ever was a people who were guided by revelation, or acknowledged of the Lord as his people, who were not hated and persecuted by the wicked and the corrupt." (*Gospel Doctrine*, p. 46.)

It must be made clear that those whom the Lord calls the honorable men and women of the earth are not being lumped in with the less than honorable. The honorable may be blinded by busyness, caught up in other causes, or preoccupied with trivia, but they do not mock the saints of God nor revile.

Significantly, Paul said he was to preach the gospel "not with wisdom of words, lest the cross of Christ be made of none effect." To preach the gospel, disdaining the jargon as well as the wisdom of the world, will often put us at variance with the intellectual ways of the world and the prevailing patterns of thought, creating another dimension of indifference, scorn, and, at least, amusement in others.

Father Lehi said of the great multitude who entered into that large and strange building, "after they did enter into that building they did point the finger of scorn at me and those that were partaking of the fruit also; but we heeded them not." (1 Nephi 8:33.) Yet while Lehi noticed the finger of scorn pointed at him (because he was doing that which was right), his response was not one of resentment; he "despised the shame of the world."

Readers will recall that in Nephi's interpretation of that vision, the great and spacious building was "the pride of the world." (1 Nephi 11:36.) Nephi described the fall thereof with this sobering note: "Thus shall be the destruction of all nations, kindreds, tongues, and people, that shall fight against the twelve apostles of the lamb." The differences between the legions representing the pride of the world and those who prefer the Lord's way are irrepressible differences.

One could scarcely expect a proud world to understand, let alone approve of, those who refuse its ways. Hence the scorn and the shame that we must all come to "despise," or care so little for, that it does not deter us from doing that which is right.

The crunches are apt to come when, because of discipleship, men persecute us, revile us, or misunderstand us. According to the Savior, some may actually go so far as to separate us from their company, holding us in disregard because of our discipleship. On occasion, sadly, competent disciples will not be chosen for certain professional chores of the world because their peers will see them as being incapacitated to perform fully because they are disciples. The only Roman "club" to which early Christians obtained admittance was the Coliseum, and, unfortunately, other guests—four-legged and hungry—had been invited too.

One has only to look at worsening conditions to realize that the regrettable trends underway will actually separate the disciples, at least behaviorally, from the mistaken majority.

When people are wrong they are reinforced in their wrong by being part of a like multitude. Perhaps it is the seeming anonymity. Perhaps they somehow feel less responsible. It was irritating and unsettling to Herod to have an articulate John the Baptist around who would not practice "if you want to get along, go along." But plain people as well as prophets irritate incorrect majorities. No wonder there is scorn and shame heaped upon those who will not go along with that which is wrong, especially when evildoers become rigidly proud of their patterns of living.

Reality does not need to prove its validity or to vouch for itself. Yet God's love, which is a part of that reality, has caused him to choose to tell us, again and again, of reality through living prophets, the living scriptures, and with the living Church to help us along the way.

Rarely do groups of people who have been so

helped (but who have often rejected this help) reach the level of honesty of those whom Samuel once addressed when he was "old and grayheaded." As Samuel rehearsed and summed up his efforts among them, noting his blamelessness, he said, "The Lord is witness against you. . . . And they answered, He is witness." Then he added, "Now therefore stand still, that I may reason with you before the Lord of all the righteous acts of the Lord, which he did to you and to your fathers." (1 Samuel 12:1-7.) So often loving prophets must wish busy people would "stand still" so that prophets could reason with them.

The same, almost tender, entreaty comes from Isaiah: "Come now, and let us reason together. . . ." (Isaiah 1:18.) Through Joseph Smith the Lord spoke of his everlasting covenant as being an evidence of his "reasoning in plainness and simplicity" to the children of men. (D&C 133:57.)

It is, to be sure, an enormous step for an individual to come to believe in "things as they really are, and things as they really will be." Reason, however, will not be enough to teach us. The Spirit must teach us and support us.

When the meridian-disciples heard from others the reports of Jesus' being resurrected, these reports were simply not convincing enough—yet Jesus had taught them well concerning the resurrection. In the sixteenth chapter of Mark we read of his appearance to Mary Magdalene and how "she went and told them that had been with him, as they mourned and wept. And they, when they had heard he was alive, and had been seen of her, believed not." (Mark 16:9-11.) Next, Jesus appeared unto two of the disciples as they walked and likewise "they went and told it unto the residue: neither believed they them." Later, when he appeared to the eleven, he upbraided them because of their "unbelief and hardness of heart, because they believed not them which had seen him after he was risen." (Mark 16:12-14.)

The point is that the resurrection was so out of the

ordinary that even extraordinary men faltered briefly before that reality of things as they really are. No wonder believers in things as they really are often have difficulty in explaining such things to disbelievers.

A loving Father has given to every individual gifts, talents, and the light of Christ. Thus that good which is done by all mortals actually grows out of the divinity in every individual, even if the person refuses to acknowledge that reality. The failure to so see this reality does not alter it. The very breath some use to deny the existence of God comes from God!

Clearly those who live a good life and serve others so well *without* being able to accept the ultimate realities of life are sons or daughters of God, and he will surely acknowledge their good deeds even if they do not now choose to acknowledge him.

Those who declare that life is without ultimate meaning are flawed in their consistency, however. How can they assert that life is absurd and then turn around and try to attach genuine meaning to any proximate cause? Of course, near-believers and doubters are in a somewhat different circumstance because they are not so declarative; they still allow for the possibility of its all being true, after all.

To be sure, disciples must build bridges of love and rapport, but at times we must be rigorous in challenging the dogmatism of disbelievers whose interior inconsistencies have implications for all of us in our shared social and political circumstances. Hence their dogmas must not be immune from scrutiny. If the ultimate realists are silent, the unrealists will only be emboldened in their errors.

A dear but disbelieving friend in an orientation session for entering freshmen at a university said, "There are no absolutes." He then paused in his speech and said quite honestly, "My goodness, I just uttered an absolute!"

Meanwhile, far be it for us to deny the reasonable pluralism that God in his love permits to exist. But there appears to be building an intellectual imperialism (with its own dogmatism); this trend grows more ominous as it seeks to ally itself with the power of the state. One of the disciple's major challenges will be to render to Caesar that which is Caesar's—but to know what to do when a swollen Caesar asks too much.

Ultimately, it is the straight and narrow way or cruel cul-de-sacs. Especially might it be said of travel on the straight and narrow way: "The use of traveling is to regulate imagination by reality, and instead of thinking how things may be, to see them as they are." (Samuel Johnson.)

Things as they really are require the believer to be at his best—to be what he really could be, and also to understand who he really is. George MacDonald said that while mankind is, alas, "always struggling to make our home in the world, we have not yet succeeded. We are not at home in it, because we are not at home with the lord of the house, the father of the family, not one with our elder brother who is his right hand." (*Life Essential*, pp. 29-30.)

No wonder the valiant and successful are those who "overcome by faith." (D&C 76:53.) All that the living Father has can only be safely entrusted to those who trust him. If we do not appreciate him, we cannot come to appreciate what he gives to us. Nor could the proven Savior be our advocate with the Father if we have not really proven ourselves in this the second estate by coping with temptations and trials such as are "common to man." (1 Corinthians 10:13.) For so the Father and Son agreed in the distant beginnings, when they planned for mankind and said of all of us, ". . . we will prove them herewith." (Abraham 3:25.) How much reality is compressed into those five terse words!

It was Alma who summed up what all informed mortals should conclude: "And now, my brethren, seeing we know these things, and they are true, let us repent, and harden not our hearts. . . ." (Alma 12:37.) Being true to what we know about things as they really are takes immense integrity and constant courage. We cannot summon up such strength by ourselves; it will take the help of the living God, the living Church, the living prophets, and the living scriptures to see us through this journey.

In the end, we will have either chosen to act in accord with things as they really are—or we will have opted for the fleeting things of this world. And this is a dying world. A living discipleship is attainable, but only if we remember that livingness begets livingness and, therefore, we stay close to the truly living things.

CHAPTER TWO

THE REALITY
OF THE
LIVING GOD

But the Lord is the true God, he is the living God, and an ever-lasting king: at his wrath the earth shall tremble, and the nations shall not be able to abide his indignation. (Jeremiah 10:10.)

And behold, he preached the word unto your fathers, and a mighty change was also wrought in their hearts, and they humbled themselves and put their trust in the true and living God. And behold, they were faithful until the end; therefore they were saved. (Alma 5:13.)

■Without, of course, the reality of the living God, there could not be the attendant realities of the living Church, nor the living prophets, nor the living scriptures.

The title of Father, or Heavenly Father, that God has chosen places us in a childlike role in relation to him, the living God. If we really accept and have even a measure of understanding of the reality of that relation-ship, then we can be counseled and corrected by him and trust him, knowing that his love and omniscience combine for our good. But if God were something other than a living Father, it would be very difficult for us to muster the necessary trust in him and to place our cares and concerns in his hands.

The great high-priestly prayer of Jesus was a prayer offered by a Son, albeit a perfect Son, to a loving, living Father. No such prayer would have been even possible if Deity were simply some "life force" or if God's stan-dards were not absolute, and if his love for us were merely relative or episodic.

Though this great reality—the living God—exists, disbelief in him seems to mount, creating a malaise in human morals. Those who disbelieve in his reality do not automatically engage in wife-beating, by any means. The decline brought on by disbelief usually is much more subtle. Without a standard of Ultimate

Truth, other standards quickly slip away. As C. S. Lewis said, "We laugh at honour and are shocked to find traitors in our midst. We castrate and then bid the geldings be fruitful." (*A Mind Awake*, p. 241.)

In a moral malaise:

Governments stunt citizens and then complain of their unheroic size.

We stop caring for our Father in heaven and then neglect aging earthly parents.

Unanchored brilliance breaks a genetic code but cannot fathom the full meaning of the Savior's sermon at Capernaum. (John 6.)

We come to prefer ten thousand regulations to the Ten Commandments.

Scientists study and then praise the order of things in the universe, marveling how it brought itself into being and ignoring the Cause of it all Who made the scientists' little puddles of knowledge possible.

In a moral malaise, society comes to tolerate certain things that would have been intolerable years before, whether these be violence or shoddiness in education. Why do so many lack the capacity to be aroused, to be stirred over such declining standards? Part of the explanation, of course, is ignorance. Part of it is indifference. But there is a new dimension to this failure of many to be aroused: intimidation growing out of the very momentum that evil has achieved. There are many mortals who fear, genuinely fear, to speak up and to lead out! It is as if a flagship were sending signals to other ships of war in a convoy, warning them, "Beware of pirates who may try to board," only to have such signals read by the sneering faces of pirates already in command on the bridges of those ships. In one American city where an effort was made to repeal ordinances benefiting homosexuals, a newspaper report told of how the petitions were turned in to a city official who is an avowed homosexual. The pirates are already on the bridge of some ships.

Fortunately for all of us, including the ungrateful,

the living God is also a loving God who has a program of repentance.

In all of this, the rule for many otherwise thoughtful people seems to be this: Ignore the obvious and the simple explanations of reality; go for something else; look beyond the living God; look "beyond the mark." If there are beings on other planets, surely they will prove to be funny-looking, like the Martians of our cartoons. Surely they will not be just more people like us, made in the image of God, who has really formed "millions of earths like this." And so it goes.

Scientists devise costly means to "speak" and "listen" to outer space, hoping for an exchange of messages from out there somewhere. The messages from outer space have come, are coming, and will come through the living God and his living prophets. To miss these messages while searching for other sounds from space is like sitting in the front row of a concert hall, straining to hear the crunch of gravel in the symphony parking lot, while missing the glorious sounds of the orchestra. How vital it is that we come to understand "things as they really are, and . . . really will be." And one of those realities is the reality of the living God.

In purely selfish terms, most of us would measure the "livingness" of God by whether or not he was very conscious of "me" and really loved "me" and had the capacity to help "me." Selfish as that is, it is one dimension of approaching the living God.

God has surely told us in enough different scriptures about how aware he is of us and of our needs. We have been told that he is so alive and aware that a sparrow cannot fall to the ground without our Father's noticing, and that the very hairs of our head are "all numbered." (Matthew 10:29-30.)

We are told that our Father in heaven knows even before we pray about that for which we will ask. (Matthew 6:8.) Jesus responded to the Pharisees on one occasion by saying "but God knoweth your hearts." (Luke 16:15.)

The Lord in a revelation for John Whitmer spoke of that which was in the latter's heart, which only the Lord and John Whitmer knew, witnessing that God was omniscient concerning the needs of that individual. (D&C 15:3.)

Paul said to the saints at Corinth, "And again, The Lord knoweth the thoughts of the wise, that they are vain." (1 Corinthians 3:20.) In the period just before the flood God saw not only the wickedness of man in the earth, but he saw also "every imagination of the thoughts" of men's hearts. (Genesis 6:5.) He knows "the things that come into your mind." (Ezekiel 11:5.) Jesus himself said before we pray, "Your father knoweth what things ye have need of." (Matthew 6:8.) Indeed, as Nephi said, "God . . . knoweth all things, and there is not anything save he knows." (2 Nephi 9:20.)

Hence omniscience is one of the characteristics of the living God. As we read in Helaman 9:41, "Except he was a God he could not know of all things." "And now, behold, you have received a witness; for if I have told you things which no man knoweth have you not received a witness?" (D&C 6:24.) God who can number sparrows and stars (the latter are too numerous, he said, for man to number) reminds us of his omniscience in this powerful scripture: "But only an account of this earth, and the inhabitants thereof, give I unto you. For behold, there are many worlds that have passed away by the word of my power. And there are many that now stand, and innumerable are they unto man; but all things are numbered unto me, for they are mine and I know them." (Moses 1:35.)

Thus, the living God *can* help us because of the perfection of his knowledge and power. He *wants* to help us because he is also made perfect in his love.

Jesus had a perfect role model in this living Father in heaven. In words that for now must surely go unappreciated by us mortals, Jesus said, "Verily, verily, I say unto you, The Son can do nothing of himself, but what he seeth the Father do: for what things soever he doeth, these also doeth the Son likewise. For the Father loveth the Son, and sheweth him all things that himself doeth: and he will shew him greater works than these, that ye may marvel." (John 5:19-20.) Someday when we understand things as they really were, that scripture can be fully appreciated.

As we deepen our worship of the living God, we encounter other deep doctrines of God that tell us more about the living God, including knowledge about things as they *were*.

The doctrine of foreordination is one of the doctrinal roads "least traveled by"; nowadays it is dealt with gently and occasionally, yet it underlines how long God has loved us and known our individual needs and capacities. It is so powerful a doctrine, however, that, isolated from other doctrines or mishandled, it can stoke the fires of fatalism, distort agency, and spill over into the perils of predestination. President Joseph Fielding Smith once warned:

> It is very evident from a thorough study of the gospel and the plan of salvation that a conclusion that those who accepted the Savior were predestined to be saved no matter what the nature of their lives must be an error. The gospel of salvation based on faithfulness and obedience to the covenants and laws of the gospel is definitely clear in the doctrines of our Lord and his inspired servants. Surely Paul never intended to convey such a thought that in the preexistence many were destined by divine decree to be saved no matter what the nature of their mortal lives might be. This might have been one of the passages in Paul's teachings which caused Peter to declare that there are in Paul's writings, "some things hard to be understood, which they that are unlearned and unstable, wrest as they do also the other scriptures, unto their own destruction." (*Improvement Era*, May 1963, pp. 350-51.)

Surely Paul, who stressed so rigorously the importance of pressing forward and running the race the full distance in our discipleship, did *not* intend a casual Christianity, in which some had won even before the race started!

Yet, though foreordination is a difficult doctrine, it

has been given to us by the living God, through living prophets, for a purpose. It can increase our understanding of how crucial this mortal second estate is and encourage us in good works. This precious doctrine can help us go the second mile because we are doubly called.

When we mortals try to comprehend rather than to accept foreordination, finite minds are trying to comprehend omniscience. A full understanding is impossible; we simply have to trust in what the Lord has told us, knowing that we are not dealing with guarantees from God, but extra opportunities and heavy responsibilities. If those responsibilities are linked to past performance or past capabilities, it should not surprise us. The Lord said, "There is a law, irrevocably decreed in heaven before the foundations of this world, upon which all blessings are predicated—And when we obtain any blessing from God, it is by obedience to that law upon which it is predicated." (D&C 130:20-21.)

That law of blessings based upon obedience prevailed in the first estate as well as in the second estate. It should not disconcert us, therefore, that the Lord has indicated that before they came here he chose some individuals to play certain roles and, therefore, these individuals have been foreordained to those assignments.

Foreordination is like any other blessing—it is a conditional bestowal subject to our faithfulness. Prophecies foreshadow events without determining those outcomes, because of a divine foreseeing of that outcome. So foreordination is a conditional bestowal of a role, responsibility, or a blessing that, likewise, foresees but does not fix the outcome.

There have been those who have failed or who have been treasonous to their trust, such as David, Solomon, and Judas. God foresaw the fall of David, but God was not the cause of it. It was David who from the balcony both saw and sent for Bathsheba. But God was not surprised by such sad developments.

24

God foresaw but did not cause Martin Harris's loss of certain pages of the translated Book of Mormon; he made plans to cope with that failure over fifteen hundred years before it was to occur. (See Preface to D&C 10, and Words of Mormon 1:6-7.)

Thus foreordination is no excuse for fatalism or arrogance or the abuse of agency. It is not, however, a doctrine that can be ignored simply because it is difficult. It is best approached, as Peter may have implied, by those who are sufficiently learned and spiritually stable. (2 Peter 3:16.)

The doctrine pertains not only to the foreordination of prophets, but also to God's precise assessment beforehand as to those who will respond to the words of the prophets and the Savior. We read these words, which came from the Savior's own lips: "I am the good shepherd, and know my sheep, and am known of mine." (John 10:14.) Similarly the Savior said, "My sheep hear my voice, and I know them, and they follow me." (John 10:27.) This could not be so without divine foreknowledge concerning all mortals and their response to the gospel—which foreknowledge is so perfect that it leaves the realm of *prediction* and enters the realm of *prophecy.*

Surely the Lord, who was able to say to his disciples, "Cast the net on the right side of the ship," knew beforehand that there were a multitude of fishes there. (John 21:6.) And if he so knew the movements and whereabouts of fishes in the little Sea of Tiberias, does it offend us that he is constantly and perfectly aware of us and our needs and that he knows beforehand which mortals will come into the gospel net?

Given these utterances in the meridian of time, it should not surprise us to have the Lord say in 1830 to the Prophet Joseph Smith, "And ye are called to bring to pass the gathering of mine elect; for mine elect hear my voice and harden not their hearts." (D&C 29:7.) The readiness of certain mortals to hear the gospel, gladly and with alacrity, is based upon their parallel responsiveness in the premortal world. No wonder the Lord could say as he did to Jeremiah, "Before I formed thee in the belly I knew thee . . . and I ordained thee a prophet unto the nations." (Jeremiah 1:5.) Paul, in writing to the saints in Rome, said, "God hath not cast away his people which he foreknew." (Romans 11:2.) He also said of God that "he hath chosen us in him before the foundation of the world." (Ephesians 1:4.)

There are clearly special cases of individuals with special limitations in life, which we cannot now fathom. Like him who was "blind from birth," some come to bring glory to God. (John 9:1-2.) We must be exceedingly careful about imputing either wrong causes or wrong rewards to all such. They are in the Lord's hands and he loves them perfectly. Some of those who have required much waiting upon in this life may be waited upon in the next world—but for the highest of reasons.

Thus when we are elected to certain mortal chores, we are elected "according to the foreknowledge of God the Father." (1 Peter 1:2.) When Abraham was advised, "thou wast chosen before thou wast born," he was among the "noble and great ones." (Abraham 3:22-23.) In the revelation given to us by President Joseph F. Smith we read that the Prophet Joseph Smith, Hyrum Smith, Brigham Young, John Taylor, Wilford Woodruff, "and other choice spirits" were also reserved by God to come forth in the fullness of times to take part in the laying of the foundations of the great latter-day work. (Joseph F. Smith—Vision 1:53.) These individuals are among the rulers that were described to Abraham centuries earlier by God. They were to be "rulers in the Church of God," not necessarily rulers in the secular kingdoms. Thus those seen by Abraham were the Spencer W. Kimballs, not the Churchills; the Pauls, not the Caesars, though obviously wise secular leaders do much lasting and commendable good.

President Joseph Fielding Smith said, "In regard to the holding of the priesthood in pre-existence, I will say that there was an organization there just as well as an organization here, and men there held authority. Men chosen to positions of trust in the spirit world held priesthood." (*Doctrines of Salvation* 3:81.)

In terms of the acceptance of the gospel and the joining of the Church, Paul said in his epistles to the saints in Corinth that (as the world measured greatness and wisdom) "not many wise men after the flesh, not many mighty, not many noble, are called." (1 Corinthians 1:26.) Thus neither the power structure nor the status structure of the world would be reproduced in the Church, though, of course, there are some happy exceptions.

Alma speaks about foreordination with great effectiveness and links it to the foreknowledge of God and perhaps even to our previous performance. (Alma 13:3-5.) The omniscience of God made it possible, therefore, for him to determine the boundaries and times of nations. (Acts 17:26; Deuteronomy 32:8.)

Elder Orson Hyde said of our life in the premortal world, "We understood things better there than we do in this lower world." He also surmised as to the agreements we made there that "it is not impossible that we signed the articles thereof with our own hands— which articles may be retained in the archives above, to be presented to us when we rise from the dead, and be judged out of our own mouths, according to that which is written in the books." Just because we have forgotten, said Elder Hyde, "our forgetfulness cannot alter the facts." Hence, the degree of detail involved in the covenants and promises we participated in at that time may be a more highly customized thing than many of us surmise. (*Journal of Discourses* 7:314-15.)

Yet, on occasion, there are inklings. President Joseph F. Smith said, "But in coming here, we forgot all, that our agency might be free indeed, to choose good or evil, that we might merit the reward of our own choice and conduct. But by the power of the Spirit, in the redemption of Christ, *through obedience, we often catch a spark from the awakened memories of the immortal soul,* which lights up

our whole being as with the glory of our former home."
(*Gospel Doctrine*, pp. 13-14. Italics added.)

As indicated earlier, this powerful teaching is bound to be puzzling in some respects, if we do not have faith and trust in the Lord. Yet if we think about it, even within our finite framework of experience, it shouldn't startle us. Mortal parents are reasonably good at predicting the behavior of their children in certain circumstances. Of this Elder James E. Talmage wrote:

> Our Heavenly Father has a full knowledge of the nature and disposition of each of His children, a knowledge gained by long observation and experience in the past eternity of our primeval childhood; a knowledge compared with which that gained by earthly parents through mortal experience with their children is infinitesimally small. By reason of that surpassing knowledge, God reads the future of child and children, of men individually and of men collectively as communities and nations; He knows what each will do under given conditions, and sees the end from the beginning. His foreknowledge is based on intelligence and reason. He foresees the future as a state which naturally and surely will be; not as one which must be because He has arbitrarily willed that it shall be. (*The Great Apostasy*, p. 20.)

Another helpful analogy is the reality that universities can and do predict with a high degree of accuracy the grades entering students will receive in their college careers based upon certain tests, past performances, etc. If mortals can do this with reasonable accuracy (even with our short span of familiarity and with finite data), surely God, the Father, who knows us perfectly, can foresee how we will respond to various challenges. Omniscience, of course, would be able to foresee with perfection what we mortals only reasonably guess at.

In all of this it is crucial, however, to remember that while we often fail our opportunities, God is neither pleased nor surprised that we do not rise to those opportunities. But we cannot say to him later on that we could have achieved had we only been given the chance. This is all part of the justice of God.

One of the most helpful—indeed necessary—insights in pondering this powerful doctrine is given in the revelation of the Lord to Moses in which the Lord says, "And all things are present with me, for I know them all." (Moses 1:6.) God does not live in the dimension of time as do we. We are not only hampered by our finiteness (experiential and intellectual), but also by being in the dimension of time. Moreover, God, since "all things are present" with him, is not simply predicting based solely on the past. In ways that are not clear to us, he *sees* rather than *foresees* the future, because all things are at once present before him.

In a revelation given through the Prophet Joseph Smith, the Lord describes himself as "the same which knoweth all things, for all things are present before mine eyes." (D&C 38:2.) From the prophet Nephi we receive the same basic insight in which we, likewise, must trust: "But the Lord knoweth all things from the beginning; wherefore, he prepareth a way to accomplish all his works among the children of men. . . ." (1 Nephi 9:6.)

We need to develop both the understanding and the trust that Mormon had when he was dealing with something that he sensed had a relationship to events yet future. He did as bidden and then made this observation: "And I do this for a wise purpose; for thus it whispereth to me, according to the workings of the Spirit of the Lord which is in me. And now, I do not know all things; but the Lord knoweth all things which are to come; wherefore, he worketh in me to do according to his will." (Words of Mormon 1:7.)

One of the dimensions of worshiping a living God is to know that he is alive and living in the sense of foreseeing. He is not a retired God whose best years are past—to whom we should pay a retroactive obeisance and whom we worship for what he has already done. He is the living God who is, at once, in the dimensions of the past and the present and the future, while we labor constrained by the limitations of time itself. Time can tug at us and play so many tricks upon us if we lack eternal perspective.

It is imperative that we always keep in mind the caveats noted earlier so that we do not indulge ourselves, or our whims, simply because of the presence of this powerful doctrine of foreordination, for with special opportunities come special responsibilities and much greater risks. The caveats include not isolating this doctrine from all the other true doctrines (such as the need to work out our salvation), not confusing it with predestination, and not attempting to explain all human circumstances thereby. We can accept God's omniscience, but we cannot comprehend it fully. But the doctrine of foreordination properly understood and humbly pursued can help us immensely in coping with the vicissitudes of life. With enlarged understanding can come an enlargement of soul. We should always understand that while God is not surprised, we may be, and that while a particular outcome is not what God would have chosen, he has clearly foreseen it.

Life's episodes may take on new meaning. For instance, was it mere happenstance that Simon, the Cyrenian, wandered into Jerusalem that very day and was pressed into service by Roman soldiers to help carry the cross of Christ? (Mark 15:21.) Simon's son, Rufus, joined the church, and was so well thought of by the apostle Paul that the latter mentioned him in his epistle to the Romans. (Romans 16:13.) Rufus was described by Paul as "chosen in the Lord." Was it, therefore, a mere accident that Simon "who passed by, coming out of the country," was asked to bear the cross of Jesus?

Properly humbled and instructed concerning the great privileges that are ours, we can cope with what seem to be very dark days; and with true perspective about "things as they really are," we can see in them a great chance to contribute. Winston Churchill, in trying to rally his countrymen in an address at Harrow School on October 29, 1941, said to them: "Do not let us speak of darker days; let us speak rather of sterner days.

These are not dark days: these are great days—the greatest days our country has ever lived; and we must all thank God that we have been allowed, each of us according to our stations, to play a part in making these days memorable in the history of our race." (Bartlett, p. 923.)

So should we regard the dispensation of the fulness of time—even when we face stern challenges and circumstances, "these are great days"! Our hearts need not fail us.

The truth about foreordination also helps us to partake of the wisdom of Alma, when he said we ought to be content with things that God has allotted to each of us. (Alma 29:3-4.) If, indeed, the things allotted to each were divinely customized according to our ability and capacity, then for us to seek to wrench ourselves free of every schooling circumstance in mortality is to tear ourselves away from matched opportunities. It is to go against divine wisdom, wisdom in which we may once have concurred before we came here and to which we once gave assent.

President Henry D. Moyle said: "I believe that we, as fellow workers in the priesthood, might well take to heart the admonition of Alma and be content with that which God hath allotted us. We might well be assured that we had something to do with our 'allotment' in our pre-existent state. This would be an additional reason for us to accept our present condition and make the best of it. It is what we agreed to do." (*Conference Report,* October 1952, p. 71.)

Surely as we draw closer to the living God, it should neither surprise us nor offend us to learn how well he knows us, nor to learn that in his matchless love he matches our capacities and our opportunities. A perfect Father would do just that!

In his infinite and perfect knowledge of us, God knows how much we need the teachings of the living prophets and the scriptures.

If we want to ask ourselves about the chief and

specific concerns of that living and loving Father in heaven, we may take our clue from how God inspired the poet-prophet Jacob. He was instructed by the Lord to write upon the plates only "a few of the things" that he considered "to be most precious," touching only lightly on "the history of this people which are called the people of Nephi."

With both space and time at a premium, Jacob then was inspired to select certain topics to inscribe upon the plates, focusing on the great revelations and prophecies "as much as it were possible, for Christ's sake and for the sake of our people." (Jacob 1:2, 4.) Therefore, Jacob selected only the "heads" of the great prophecies and revelations. The word *heads* implies that these were to be the headlines, highlights, or major teachings. A spiritual summary was necessary because too much detail could not be placed in the plates.

What do we see then in the remaining chapters of the book of Jacob as to the topics so selected?

Jacob expressed the desire to persuade all men not to rebel against God, but to believe in Christ and to suffer Christ's cross and "bear the shame of the world." (1:8.)

Then, drawing upon the growing sexual immorality of his people, Jacob made his classic denunciation of unchastity and unfaithfulness. (Chapter 2.)

Jacob also warned of materialism and of his people's intensified search for gold and silver (2:12), which, ironically, led to a persecution of those who were poor. He urged his brethren to share and to "think of your brethren like unto yourselves, and be familiar with all and free with your substance, that they may be rich like unto you." (2:17.)

Again, he denounced pride and unchastity and noted the terrible consequences of unchastity with regard to tender wives and children. (2:35.) He praised the Lamanites for their comparative righteousness and commended them for fidelity in marriage as he warned his own people against lasciviousness. (3:5-12.)

Next, Jacob noted how the law of Moses among the Nephites was to point them to Christ. (Chapter 3.) He reassured his listeners and readers that God shows us our weaknesses so that we can realize that it is by his grace that we have power to do things. (3:7.) He urged each of us to be reconciled unto God through the atonement of Christ. (3:11.) He described how the Spirit gives us the truth of things as they really are and as they really will be. (3:13.)

Jacob then bemoaned what happened to the Jews who "sought for things they could not understand," and who came to be constantly "looking beyond the mark" because they craved complexity. (3:14.) He prophesied the rejection of Jesus by the Jews. (3:14.)

Jacob devoted nearly two chapters to quoting the prophet Zenos and the allegory of the tame and wild olive tree denoting Israel and the gentiles, and to the pruning of the vineyard, as he expanded upon the allegory of the olive tree. (Chapters 5 and 6.)

In chapter 7, the final chapter of Jacob's account, we have the encounter with Sherem, the antichrist, in which Jacob came off conqueror. (7:25.)

Finally, Jacob concluded his portion of the Book of Mormon by saying that he had done his best in this life, "that the time passed away with us, and also our lives passed away like as it were unto us a dream, we being a lonesome and a solemn people, wanderers, cast out from Jerusalem, born in tribulation, in a wilderness, and hated of our brethren, which caused wars and contentions; wherefore, we did mourn out our days." (Jacob 7:26.)

The topics Jacob chose to stress in his last lecture were the "heads" of great prophecies and the great revelations, the things that matter most. He stressed those realities which the living God wanted, once again, to be underscored.

We see how the living God, operating through the living prophet, will stress the weightier matters, the things that we most need to pay attention to. But we see also how the living prophet will rise to the particular challenges within his environment, as Jacob did with regard to gross unchastity.

The more we pray, ponder, and strive to live righteously, the more we see the very remarkable interplay of the living God with living prophets, the living Church, and the living gospel. Anything less than this combination would not permit us to have an abundant life now and exaltation (with perpetuity of individual personality), which is *really* living in the world to come.

A story is told of two Texans: one a millionaire who decreed in his will that he would be buried in his white Cadillac, the other a gravedigger. As the Cadillac coffin was lowered into the grave carrying the departed millionaire's body, the envious gravedigger watched that spectacle of opulence and said, "Man, that's really living!" We can make the same mistake of perspective by not seeing things as they really are.

In the fundamental division of the things created by God there were "things to act and things to be acted upon." (2 Nephi 2:14.) The former, mankind, were to "act for themselves and not to be acted upon." (2 Nephi 2:26.) The more we sin, the more we are acted upon, eventually coming to be almost like inanimate objects that are acted upon. Thus it is that living, really living, is irrevocably tied to personal righteousness. It is the same with freedom; only the righteous are fully free. Each wrong choice, which we freely make, makes us less free and more acted upon. Yet those who complain of the seeming constraints of the straight and narrow way do not see this reality. Ironically, those who are made less and less free by successive sinning taunt those on the Lord's path, who know the personal liberty of righteousness. It would be comic if it were not so tragic.

Sensitivity to sin, rather than timidity, is the mark of great courage and wisdom. It is the courage and savvy of the mountain climber who knows the risks of a loose rock, who shuns the easy route and thus avoids the craggy cul-de-sac, and who knows that the way up is the way out. Such a climber is not afraid to be careful. He will gladly tie himself to safe companions, and will hang on with them in the midst of fierce winds.

It is very nettling to be reminded by the living God, through living prophets, the living scriptures, and the living Church, of one's unfinished work and of one's remaining possibilities. The living God reinforces his promptings by our consciences; the living prophets particularize painfully; the living Church lays heavy duties and responsibilities upon us; the living scriptures add to the stimuli, for the word of God can scarcely be opened without giving us a start, suggesting something that needs to be done or undone. So much livingness does not seem to leave much room for repose.

But could we honestly worship the living God or care much about membership in the living Church if it all were not really so? If having faith were just a casual, rhetorical game to be gone through periodically, we would scarcely be changed by it all. Worse, the human condition would be entirely hopeless.

When we not only accept the existence of God but also begin to worship him and to follow him, all sorts of things happen in our lives and, through us, in the lives of others. Yet disbelievers are often either "angry with God for not existing" or "equally angry with Him for creating a world." (Lewis, A Mind Awake, p. 62.) There are others, of course, who accept the existence of God, but who smugly do not choose to take him seriously.

Others believe their morals are superior to God's. Because he does not adopt their issues or jump the hurdles they wish him to jump, they are not going to extend themselves in worship of him. The Lord describes such individuals as "walking in darkness at noon-day." (D&C 95:6.) The living God will not be disregarded.

So many others settle down in a comfortable creed that periodically focuses on a god who does little and who demands little: "He is there if you wish for Him, like a book on a shelf. He will not pursue you." (Lewis,

A Mind Awake, p. 62.) It was Isaiah who declaimed those people who "regard not the work of the Lord, neither consider the operation of his hands." (Isaiah 5:12.)

The living God, however, because he is a loving God, works to polish his prophets as well as his people. The Prophet Joseph Smith's description of himself (given in two different images) is very striking. On one occasion he described himself as a huge, uncut stone that needed to be trimmed and polished by having edges knocked off here and there by the experiences of life. (HC 5:401.) In the other figure, he describes himself as wont to swim in deep water, and says that difficult experiences had almost become "a second nature to me." (D&C 127:2.)

The living God never leaves us alone even when we seek to move away from him. When the living God called Jonah to go to Nineveh, the prophet, out of fear of men, strove to go to Tarshish instead. The living God was not busy elsewhere or slumbering; he delivered Jonah unceremoniously to Nineveh! That is the sort of thing the living God does.

A passive life force or an indulgent grandfather God wouldn't worry about that sort of detail—as long as we are being basically good boys and girls who might find some good to do in Tarshish. But we have a precise and loving Father in heaven who knows what we need and who loves us enough to get us to Nineveh instead of settling for the chores of Tarshish.

We keep forgetting that a test must really be a test, and a trial, a trial. We forget too that when these come to us they are carefully shaped to wring us and to wrench us. It is a measure of both the love of a living God and his perfect awareness of our needs. In our hearts we often know this—even if we resent it!

There are other challenges that may puzzle us, however. We can't figure them out. Could it be that Father has customized chores for us to do in the eternities and therefore chooses to give us now a growth experience we do not seem to need—but that he knows we need? He knows what is missing from our storehouse of self-esteem, because his inventory of that storehouse has been going on for a long, long time. We have just done the little spot-checking lately and merely surmise where the shortages are.

When those who call themselves realists urge us to yield to the temptations of the flesh, because everybody's doing it or because that's how things are, the living God (through the living prophets, Church, and scriptures) reminds us, not of how things seem to be, but of how things really are. The genuine realist is really able to "consider the lilies in the field" and thereby see a planning and a providing God in marvelous microcosm—or he can consider the heavens and see God moving in majestic and marvelous macrocosm! (D&C 84:82; 88:47.)

The Lord speaks of our responsibility to "wise men and rulers" who need to "hear and know that which they have never considered." (D&C 101:94.) When we bring added light to people, we bring them added realism, not less, without which some live midst the lilies without noticing, and merely glance at the galaxies; the pattern of their lives keeps them from seeing divine design all about them. (2 Nephi 15:12.)

Detractors may say that just believing in the living God does not necessarily make a man a better father. The answer is that it will do so if he *really* believes, because all he comes to know through the living scriptures about the living God (as the living Father) will touch him deeply in his soul. The change will probably not occur in the twinkling of an eye, but the more he knows about his Holy Father, the more he will want to become better himself. Someone who does not believe in the living God but who is a reasonably good father would be even better if he believed in and followed a living God.

If we examine the rigorous and exclusive experience our loving Heavenly Father designed for his Only

Begotten Son, which included Gethsemane and Calvary, we can see that this loving and living God will stretch our souls too, if we will but let him. And what would we really think of such a God if he were not doing this? Disinterest is no part of Divinity.

Knowing as we do that we agreed beforehand to these earthly experiences (including the condition that we would have our memories dimmed, if not obliterated, so that the growing experience could be complete), how would we really feel later on if the living God were to tell us that, in the midpassage of his plan, he became so sorry for us that he couldn't go through with it—the very plan that, when it was originally outlined, we as his sons and daughters rejoiced over? We might better understand God, but we would scarcely worship him! His plan is not something that can be called off.

The fact remains that, whether or not we admit it, we are counting on God's being a God, even if we fail to measure up as his sons and daughters!

The living God not only stays with his plan, but also with his standards. The injunction given in the Sacred Grove to Joseph Smith at the time of the Restoration is totally consistent with the character and standards of Jesus at the time he was here in his earthly ministry in the Holy Land. The Savior condemned the errors in both behavior and doctrine that had grown up in ancient Judaism; later he did the same regarding supposed Christianity. It shouldn't surprise us if he still condemns doctrinal falsity or casualness today. If Jesus of Nazareth described the way as straight and narrow (with few finding it), could he endorse the broad way with hundreds of competing and disagreeing Christian churches? Could he, who was baptized to fulfill all righteousness, a few centuries later condone alleged programs of salvation that do not regard baptism by immersion with authority as essential?

The living prophets, if they seem monotonous, are simply reporting what they know from the living God.

The fact that it is essentially the same message from dispensation to dispensation merely confirms the truth of such utterances. Monotony does not lessen verity. We may grow tired of hearing that the earth is round, but our boredom will not change its shape.

Really trusting in the living Lord includes trusting his timing. The woman of Canaan sensed that Jesus was a special being. Nevertheless, she was told by the Savior himself that he was "not sent but unto the lost sheep of the house of Israel." (Matthew 15:24.) This must indeed have been a difficult declaration to receive even with the miracle that ensued. After all, it was years later that the church, with Paul designated as the Apostle to the Gentiles, took the gospel to the gentiles. And it was to be centuries, indeed not until our time, before Jesus' instructions to preach the gospel to all nations would begin to be carried out.

What of those individuals or peoples who are caught in these time troughs, whether the troughs be of short or lengthy duration? Not surprisingly, the merciful Lord who designed those troughs has said in modern revelation that "all who would have received [the gospel] with all their hearts" will be given a clear chance so to do in the spirit world. (Joseph Smith—Vision 1:8.) If they do accept, they will have all the blessings that would have been theirs had they accepted the fullness of the gospel in their second estate.

Thus we are often confronted with situations in which certain things will be—someday, but not now. For instance, the coming of consecration with its own laws and economic system has been foretold, but the implementation is not yet. Meanwhile, we are to pay our tithes and offerings in what is yet another example of things as they will become but are not yet.

But this divine unfolding of things that will be is not a divine unraveling. We have been told that God cannot lie. (Titus 1:2.) The time will never come when that reality changes. Likewise, we have been taught that "wickedness never was happiness." (Alma 41:10.) In the unfolding referred to, wickedness never will become happiness.

Continuing revelation and God's plan that it parallels is like the timely unfolding of a huge tapestry. Those of us who live out our lives seeing mostly one segment of that tapestry must not mistake what we see for the whole of the tapestry. It is the same with the unfolding of the kingdom. The enemies of the church thought the killings at Carthage would be a "period," ending the restored Church. But Carthage was really a "comma." Still earlier, the grimness and the grisliness of the crucifixion at Golgotha so overcame some early disciples that a few went "a fishing." (John 21:3.) What they could not fully realize in their grief growing out of Golgotha was that there would be, almost momentarily, a further unfolding that would bring into their view the glory of the resurrection—which had never before been seen or witnessed!

The disciple must be in a posture of constant anticipation, and yet he can have the serenity and security of knowing that the unfolding he is experiencing is part of a glorious pattern set from before the foundations of the world by the living God.

One cannot believe in the living God whom the living scriptures describe and who is spoken about by living prophets, and still not come to understand too that there is also a devil. The italicized words in the phrases that follow emphasize that we are told about the devil by living prophets and by the Lord.

We are told, for instance, that the adversary will attempt to appear "as an *angel of light.*" (2 Corinthians 11:14.) Does that not tell us much about his secret yearnings as well as his stratagems?

He is referred to by the Lord as "that old serpent," suggesting how we cannot take the adversary's capacity for cunning very lightly. (D&C 88:110.) We are told that he *"rebelled* against God." His rebellion followed his rejection in premortal councils, and the anger seems to deepen in him with the passage of time. (D&C 76:28.)

We are reminded that "Satan seeketh to *destroy.*" (D&C 132:57.) We are reminded also that there will be a period when Satan is *bound,* and that will be the same moment when "time is no longer." (D&C 84:100.)

We are reminded that Satan has the capacity to put things into our *hearts* if we are not righteous, but we are told that he does *not* have power to *tempt* little children. (D&C 63:28; 29:47.)

God will protect us against an overload of temptations from the adversary, so that we are *not tempted above that which we are able to bear;* there will always be a way to escape if, indeed, we are searching for it. (1 Corinthians 10:13.)

We are reminded that the adversary "thinketh to *overpower*" our testimony. (D&C 10:33.)

The adversary has busied himself in *founding* a church—his perpetual pattern of trying to find substitutes. (1 Nephi 14:3.)

The adversary covenants to *"combine against all righteousness."* (3 Nephi 6:28.) There will be *combinations* built up by the devil *to overthrow freedom.* (Ether 8:25.) He is still acting out against the principle of freedom. We are reminded of the endless misery in the kingdom of the devil whose inhabitants, along with him, will fret again and again over what might have been.

Concerning the power of the devil we read how *inequalities* among men come *because of sin.* (Alma 28:13.) Has the reader seen any marches and placards lately protesting the inequalities arising out of sin? Do not stay at your window waiting for that parade!

How quickly he moves in even where people have had special spiritual experiences, seeking to get people who have seen signs *"to disbelieve all which they had heard and seen."* (3 Nephi 2:1-2.) The adversary has a better chance to persuade us that what we believe is foolish if we worry about looking foolish in front of our fellowmen. We read about the subtleties of the devil and that the adversary *persuadeth not one man to do good.* (Alma 12:4; Moroni 7:17.)

He *cheateth* people's souls; and having thus persuaded people that there is no devil, he becomes a *shepherd of many.* (2 Nephi 28:21-22; Alma 5:39.)

He "*will not support his children at the last day.*" (Alma 30:60.) We are told he could *never have power* over men *if they lived like Moroni.* (Alma 48:17.)

Because *he is so angry* himself, he is always *stirring people up to anger.* (Moroni 9:3.) There are many people today who live at the edge of violence; ruffle them ever so slightly, and they move into actual violence.

Satan's fatal flaw was that Satan "*knew not the mind of God.*" (Moses 4:6.) Nor, apparently, did he care to find out about the will of God. He had his own plans and desires. Thus the son of the morning "was angry." (Abraham 3:28.) Because he is miserable, he *desires that all men might be miserable* like unto himself. (2 Nephi 2:18.)

We learn that he "*sought to take the kingdom* of our God and his Christ." (D&C 76:28.) Lucifer rebelled against Jesus much as Cain rebelled against Abel, but the Author of liberty could not let the adversary prevail in premortal councils nor can he let him prevail now. (D&C 76:25.) Only *we* can let him prevail in our lives. It is up to us.

How tragic it is that so many mortals are mercenaries for the adversary; that is, they do his bidding and are hired by him—bought off at such low prices. A little status, a little money, a little praise, a little fleeting fame, and they are willing to do the bidding of him who can offer all sorts of transitory "rewards," but who has no celestial currency. It is amazing how well the adversary has done; his mercenaries never seem to discover the self-destructive nature of their pay and the awful bankruptcy of their poor paymaster!

The hundreds of references in scripture concerning the adversary have been given to us for a purpose. When we accept the reality of Jesus and the living Father in heaven, we also must accept the reality of Satan!

James gives us great counsel: If we resist the devil he will flee from us. (James 4:7.) But as Paul warned, if we "give place" to the devil instead of for a portion of God's words (Alma 32:27), we have made a basic decision in life (Ephesians 4:27). We may not give adequate priority to the great and grand central realities, but the adversary is very active in trying to dissuade us of these. President David O. McKay taught that "Satan . . . is active and is prompting at this moment the denial of God's existence, of the existence of his Beloved Son, and denying the efficacy of the gospel of Jesus Christ." (*Conference Report*, October 1965, p. 9.) He knows the difference between what is central and what is peripheral!

Thus is a fugitive and a vagabond who has alienated himself proceeding to alienate all of our Father's children whom he can. Whereas the living God seeks to share his joy, the miserable one seeks to share his misery. (2 Nephi 2:18.)

The adversary is much less interested in making of us physical clones than he is in converting us into behavioral clones. Truly, the stunning sameness of gross sinners ought to be enough to frighten anyone who really cares for freedom and individuality. Poor Satan—it can't be much fun being a cheerleader for a chorus of clones, but how he stays at his task!

The living God governs the galaxies, yet he came to a grove in 1820 and called an obscure farm boy by his first name—"Joseph." The living Lord reminded Jeremiah that before Jeremiah was born the Lord ordained him a prophet. When he who has created worlds without number can relate to men with such personalized precision, we are seeing the living God in action. Far from playing a cosmic game of hide-and-seek with man, the living God "doeth that which is good among the children of men; and he doeth nothing save it be plain unto the children of men; and he inviteth them all to come unto him and partake of his goodness; and he denieth none that come unto him, black and white, bond and free, male and female; and he remembereth the heathen; and all are alike unto God, both Jew and Gentile." (2 Nephi 26:33.)

His perfection is a pleading perfection. He is a commending as well as a commanding God. Only a living God would sacrifice his Only Begotten Son so that we might be spared from everlasting death.

CHAPTER THREE

THE REALITY OF THE LIVING CHURCH

But seek ye first the kingdom of God, and his righteousness; and all these things shall be added unto you. (Matthew 6:33, King James Translation.)

Wherefore, seek not the things of this world but seek ye first to build up the kingdom of God, *and to establish his righteousness,* and all these things shall be added unto you. (Matthew 6:38, Joseph Smith Translation. [Additional words emphasized.])

■A living prophet, Joseph Smith, gave to us the full and inspired translation of the words of the Savior so that, among other things, we would know that the kingdom of the living God is not merely a loose confederacy of believers. The living Church was and is a real kingdom, with a king, authority, ordinances, rules, doctrines, and duties. The heresy of a Christianity without the Savior's church is one of the worst but most successful heresies of history. If we do not understand the reality of the living Church, we do not know the truth of things as they really are.

The utterance of the Savior cited at the beginning of this chapter has a strong institutional flavor. This statement, preserved by Matthew, must be juxtaposed with the revelation of 1830 in which Christ said that The Church of Jesus Christ of Latter-day Saints was "the only true and living church upon the face of the whole earth." (D&C 1:30.) This was, and is, a designation so significant that the key words contained within it must not be passed over lightly.

The word *only* asserts a uniqueness and singularity about The Church of Jesus Christ of Latter-day Saints as the exclusive ecclesiastical, authority-bearing agent for our Father in heaven in this dispensation.

Had the Lord said *the* Church is *a* true and living church (or if the name given had been *A* Church of

Jesus Christ of Latter-day Saints), this would have implied there are other fully acceptable alternatives available to man. Thus what was said by the Lord in 1830, not surprisingly, was consistent with the instructions given in the grove to Joseph Smith in 1820; the answer to Joseph's prayer about which church to join was, "Join none of them."

When the Lord used the designation "true," he implied that the doctrines of the Church and its authority are not just partially true, but true as measured by divine standards. The Church is not, therefore, conceptually compromised by having been made up from doctrinal debris left over from another age, nor is it comprised of mere fragments of the true faith. It is based upon the *fullness* of the gospel of him whose *name* it bears, thus passing the two tests for proving his church that were given by Jesus during his visit to the Nephites. (3 Nephi 27:8.)

When the word *living* is used, it carries a divinely deliberate connotation. The Church is neither dead nor dying, nor is it even wounded. The Church, like the living God who established it, is alive, aware, and functioning. It is not a museum that houses a fossilized faith; rather, it is a kinetic kingdom characterized by living faith in living disciples.

Indeed, a prophecy from the Lord describes his church as an expanding church, as the Lord's army, that is to become numerically "very great." Surely a diminishing, shrinking church is not the kingdom Daniel foresaw that was to have small beginnings (the stone cut out of the mountain without hands) but that eventually would fill the whole earth. (Daniel 2:35, 44-45. Compare Daniel 2:44 and D&C 105:32.) Nor is the Lord's temple to be built by an unsought-for church; what Isaiah and Micah viewed was "the mountain of the Lord's house," drawing people from *all* nations. (Isaiah 2:2; Micah 4:1.)

The living Church is one that responds to stimuli, that has movement, and that has the capacity to reproduce itself.

The Church of Jesus Christ of Latter-day Saints is, in fact, the living Church.

Elder Boyd K. Packer has observed of the endorsing words in the 1830 revelation (D&C 1:30), "Now this is not to say that the churches, all of them, are without some truth. They have some truth—some of them have very much of it. They have a form of godliness. Often the clergy and adherents are not without dedication, and many of them practice remarkably well the virtues of Christianity. They are, nonetheless, incomplete."

Elder Packer likened the living Church to the keyboard of a piano, which is capable of giving us "variety without limits" "to suit every mood and satisfy every need." He then said: "How disappointing when the fullness of the gospel, the whole keyboard, is here upon the earth, that many churches tap on a single key. The note they stress may be essential to complete harmony of religious experience, but it is, nonetheless, not all there is, it isn't the fullness." (*Ensign*, December 1971, pp. 40-41.)

In one long-established nation of Christianity, other churches have closed down, sold, or boarded up five hundred of their chapels in just the last five years. In that same land, The Church of Jesus Christ of Latter-day Saints currently has fifteen buildings under construction and another twenty in the site-selection or planning stages.

The fact that some other churches should find themselves thus failing is not necessarily something to rejoice over, because, among other things, it means that insofar as those churches once involved their members with the scriptures, now, to quote Elder Packer, "We face the frightening thought of a generation raised without any contact with scripture." (Ibid.)

The true and living Church would need to be sufficiently independent of other mortal institutions doctrinally, financially, and as to its authority, as well as for other reasons. (D&C 78:13-14.) One of those reasons is so that God's standards can be objectively applied to world circumstances and to all individuals. C. S. Lewis observed, "Unless the measuring rod is independent of the things measured, we can do no measuring. . . ." (*A Mind Awake,* p. 36.) No wonder Paul described the Church of the living God as "the pillar and ground of the truth." (1 Timothy 3:15.) The living Church will uphold the Savior's standards when many others shrink from those standards!

The very divinity of the standards that come to us from the living God (and of which we are reminded by the living prophets and the living scriptures) must be taught and administered by the living Church based on a knowledge "of things as they really are and of things as they really will be."

The living Church, an independent church, can perform that service for mankind, but a dying church, or any church based upon the philosophies of men, could have no objective measuring standard outside itself by which human behavior can be gauged and hopefully corrected. Policies or doctrines that mirror the attitudinal majority of a given age become the commandments of men. (D&C 46:7; Matthew 15:9.) Unsurprisingly, the churches of men will inevitably preach the commandments of men, seasoned with some scripture, preferably of modern translation.

From the early 1800s when interdenominational strife and competition was so intense that young Joseph Smith was made uneasy thereby, we have drifted very far, even into circumstances in which many denominations—far from being rigid doctrinally—are competing for popularity in an increasingly secularized society by diluting or democratizing basic doctrines. Others are using what energy and commitment are available to hold on to what congregations they have.

There is today more ecumenicism, but there is also more shared doubt. More and more people believe less and less—but they do believe it together. The fewer the issues, the easier it is to get agreements. The fewer standards there are, the less there is for congregations to rebel against.

Since knowing is tied to doing, and doing to knowing, there is an awful cycle in all of this. Jesus said we can know of the divinity of his doctrines by keeping his commandments and by doing the will of the Father. Therefore, a slackening of behavioral standards brings more doubt. (John 7:16-17.) Such doubters will not want to be reminded of the strong, true doctrines pertaining to human behavior. Standards will grow even more slack, and true teachings will dwindle even further.

But God's doctrines were given to bring men closer to him. Modifications attempted by men may seem to bring them closer to each other, but they will be more and more distant from their Father in heaven!

Statistics are not the full measure of the living Church, but since living implies growing, it is interesting to note that The Church of Jesus Christ of Latter-day Saints (which required one hundred years to create its first one hundred stakes) began in 1978 to create one hundred new stakes a year. Convert baptism levels, though far from what they should and will be, are the highest ever, and the corps of full-time missionaries carrying the Master's message to many nations is by far the largest such corps in the history of the Church.

Several temples are under planning or construction—another marked fulfillment of prophecy, for modern prophets have said the day would come when there would be many temples operating virtually night and day. The true and living Church now has some five hundred chapels or stake centers under construction, with several hundred on the drawing boards.

With the June 1978 revelation concerning the extension of the privileges of priesthood and temple blessings, Isaiah 2 can now be completely fulfilled: "And it shall come to pass in the last days, that the mountain of the Lord's house shall be established in the top of the mountains, and shall be exalted above the hills; and all nations shall flow unto it." Likewise, the Church is growing in nations within which men and women will be raised up as laborers of the eleventh hour in the

Lord's vineyard (Matthew 20:1-16), persons who will be able to lead and direct his affairs just as foreseen: "For behold, the Lord doth grant unto all nations, of their own nation and tongue, to teach his word, yea, in wisdom, all that he seeth fit that they should have; therefore we see that the Lord doth counsel in wisdom, according to that which is just and true." (Alma 29:8.)

Through the use of technology and ways and means not now clear to us, we will see a complete fulfillment of Doctrine and Covenants 90:11: "For it shall come to pass in that day, that *every man* shall *hear* the fulness of the gospel in his own tongue, and in his own language, through those *who are ordained unto this power*, by the administration of the Comforter, shed forth upon them for the revelation of Jesus Christ." (Italics added.)

It is noteworthy that scripture says that men shall *hear* the gospel, suggesting, along with the scope of the spread of the gospel, that those mortals who either do not have the benefit of a written language or who are not literate will still, through technology and other means, be able to hear the gospel.

Yet many do not respond to the living gospel preached by the living Church. Is it possible that the very plainness and simplicity of the gospel of Jesus Christ as carried forward by the living Church figure somehow in the narrowness and straightness of the way and also in the fact that few there be that find it? Can it be so, when the way out of the human predicament is also the way into the kingdom of heaven? Apparently.

The desensitizing effect of sin closes up the portals of perception so that the narrow way cannot be seen by those being led so carefully in an opposite direction.

The seeming obscurity and unfashionability of the living Church and the seeming improbability of its message are likewise contributing factors to the un-likelihood of some persons' discovering the way. The way is surely not to be found by watching the surge of the crowd for direction.

Suffice it to say, nonreaders of the scriptures are less

apt to find the way, for the living scriptures lead to the living Church. Those who are too caught up with the cares of the world will be too busy to search. It is not a way we will find by looking for a route that is easy to travel. The straight way is, in fact, not only narrow, but it also is a way filled with some deterrents, like chastisement. (D&C 95:1.) It is not something that is casual and meandering; it is straight. Forces may even combine to "hedge up the way." (D&C 122:7.)

It is not a route or a corridor to be found by those who insist on walking in their own way (D&C 1:16); rather, it takes a broad way and a wide gate to accommodate all those converging souls who think of themselves as walking so heroically in their own way.

The straight and narrow way is marked by required ordinances that may deflect the so-called free spirits, especially such ordinances as baptism and eternal marriage. Ordinances sound so old-fashioned, like the cross!

The heresy of churchless Christians goes hand in hand with the heresy of a relaxed or retired god. In such circumstances, ordinances would be unwanted reminders of still other marks and requirements of the living Church. If there must be ritual let it be occasional. If there must be sermons, let them focus on the issues of the day. If there must be ordinances, let them be optional for those who feel they need that sort of primitive thing.

Little wonder that in such settings there is a genuine reluctance by some of the cloth to jar adherents out of their own life-style. Thus undisturbed, individuals can all walk in their own ways and, at the same time, feel they belong to a church. Thus lulled, there would be reluctance to speak of narrow things like the narrow way. If necessary, best take one's thoughts away from personal reform and direct them to societal reforms for real relevance. Why is it that for many persons changing others is so exciting and so relevant, while changing oneself is so boring and irrelevant?

Of course the Jews would have been very keen about Jesus of Nazareth if he had been interested in the relevance of rescuing them from Rome. The majority regarded sermons on the mount as no substitute for political action!

It is instructive to compare the Savior's words in the New Testament and in the Book of Mormon with added revelation concerning the straightness and the narrowness of the way.

In the New Testament we read:

> Enter ye in at the strait gate: for wide is the gate, and broad is the way, that leadeth to destruction, and many there be which go in thereat: Because strait is the gate, and narrow is the way, which leadeth unto life, and few there be that find it. (Matthew 7:13-14.)

The Book of Mormon tells us:

> Enter ye in at the strait gate; for strait is the gate, and narrow is the way that leads to life, and few there be that find it; but wide is the gate, and broad the way which leads to death, and many there be that travel therein, until the night cometh, wherein no man can work. (3 Nephi 27:33.)

And in modern revelation we read:

> For strait is the gate, and narrow the way *that leadeth unto the exaltation and continuation of the lives,* and few there be that find it, *because ye receive me not in the world, neither do ye know me. But if ye receive me in the world, then shall ye know me, and shall receive your exaltation: that where I am ye shall be also.* (D&C 132:22-23. Words added in the modern revelation are italicized.)

The significant additions in the Doctrine and Covenants make clear what was not revealed earlier, at least to the multitudes.

Those people do not find the way who do not receive Jesus in the world or who do not really come to know him. Modern revelation aids us so very much in this verse of scripture, just as it does in the inspired rendering of Matthew 6:33. (See scriptures at beginning of this chapter.)

Another example of revelation by amplification occurs in the scripture, "For many are called, but few are chosen." (Matthew 22:14, King James Version.) The Doctrine and Covenants amplifies this text as follows (with additional words in italics):

> Behold, there are many called, but few are chosen. *And why are they not chosen? Because their hearts are set so much upon the things of this world, and aspire to the honors of men, that they do not learn this one lesson—That the rights of the priesthood are inseparably connected with the powers of heaven, and that the powers of heaven cannot be controlled nor handled only upon the principles of righteousness.* (D&C 121:34-36.)

Under such careful strictures, if the servants of the Lord were to pretend that there is another way, this would be gross deception and betrayal. There is "none other way." (2 Nephi 9:41; 31:21; Mosiah 3:17.)

The straight and narrow way referred to above has to do with salvation and exaltation, but there is a related analogy in the scriptures in which we read the following: "And the Lord said unto Moses, Make thee a fiery serpent, and set it upon a pole: and it shall come to pass, that every one that is bitten, when he looketh upon it, shall live." (Numbers 21:8.)

In the Book of Mormon we have added information about that very episode: "And he did straiten them in the wilderness with his rod; for they hardened their hearts, even as ye have; and the Lord straitened them because of their iniquity. He sent fiery flying serpents among them; and after they were bitten he prepared a way that they might be healed; and the labor which they had to perform was to look; and *because of the simpleness of the way, or the easiness* of it, there were many who perished." (1 Nephi 17:41. Italics added.)

The seeming simpleness or easiness of physical salvation in the case of those who had been bitten by the fiery, flying serpents was, strangely enough, a deterrent even in the face of death. The same deterrent of simpleness and easiness will deflect some who are not true seekers after eternal life. Even when things are going well, some do not seek or thank God. As George Mac-

Donald observed: "To trust in Him when no need is pressing, when things seem going right of themselves, may be harder than when things seem going wrong." (*Anthology*, p. 124.)

The prophets of God who lead the living Church prefer simpleness and plainness because of the great importance of what they are communicating. They want to minimize the words and thus minimize the risks of not communicating effectively. Alas, those hearers who prefer complexity and sophistication often do so because they are seeking a way out, not a way in!

People who despise plainness are apt to despise the prophets because prophets speak plainly. People can become absorbed in sophisticated and complex things just so long before they become blind to the simple things. People who are looking beyond the mark will miss seeing what they most need to see. They will finally get the desires of their heart and will be delivered over to things "they cannot understand, because they desired it." (Jacob 4:14.) How important, by contrast, it is for us to desire to be taught by the Spirit so that we can understand "things as they really are and as they really will be."

People who look beyond the mark are clearly not without sight. They can see, but it is what they choose to look at (or for) that causes a lack of vision. It might be likened to anxiously watching a traffic light two intersections away and missing an oncoming truck in our own intersection; or a basketball player taking his eyes off the basket and missing an easy layup because he glances at a hotdog vendor in the stands; or the blindness of the British fortifying Singapore prior to World War II with mighty guns firing only seaward as the Japanese came by land; or those who were too busy staring in search of a political liberator and missed the Messiah.

Simplicity requires plain language; and the more eroded and less precise language becomes, the less it communicates. Bureaucratic language in modern government is a classic example of this. When we don't like to face up to hard facts, we use soft words. We do not speak about killing a baby within the womb, but about the "termination of potential life." Words are often multiplied to try to cover dark deeds.

The living Church can, to a great extent, provide us with growth experiences we would not otherwise have through added friendships. It is true, for instance, that the Latter-day Saint has immediate friends, or "instant community," in every country or city to which he would go where there are already brothers and sisters in the gospel. He has a chance to become a native rather than being a mere tourist.

Likewise, institutional life in the Church gives us a chance not only to come to grips with our own deficiencies, but also, as appropriate, to help others with theirs. We seem to take turns being hammer and anvil when we are not the actual object being shaped. The living Church gives us experience not only in personal repentance, but also in seeing and assisting in the progress and repentance of others. The common commitment to the living God and the living prophet and the living Church—along with the common commitment to living scriptures—creates in us a will to work things out, facilitating cooperation on a much larger and deeper scale than would otherwise be the case.

In the living Church we can even learn to do good without growing weary. Perhaps one of the reasons we sometimes weary of well doing is that the expected expressions of appreciation are not always forthcoming. What our own ingratitude does not teach us about that particular sin, we are apt to learn from the occasional ingratitude of others toward us. The resilience and generosity of Joseph in Egypt is a constant marvel. He helped to reinstate the Pharaoh's deposed chief butler by interpreting the butler's dream, asking only of the butler that he would "think on me when it shall be well with thee. . . . Yet did not the chief butler remember Joseph, but forgat him." (Genesis 40:14, 23.) We do not read of Joseph's being bitter then or ever, though he had so many chances to do so.

We are, said the Savior, to lend and to "do good . . . hoping for nothing" in return; then we can become "children of the Highest: for he is kind unto the unthankful." (Luke 6:35.) Where, Jesus asked, were the other nine lepers he had healed, since only one was grateful enough to come back? (Luke 17:17.) Jesus noted but did not rail at the lack of appreciation in the ninety percent.

So it must be with us. We like gratitude to be expressed so that it can be heard of men. We do not like waiting for deferred payments, for the "now" that is in us dies so slowly. We like others to know in full what trouble we have gone to for them, with all the clinical details. But if they were to relive and to feel fully what our giving has cost us, it would cost them, too; it would no longer be our gift to them. The living Church can help us meet such challenges.

The disciple is expected to give appreciation always and to be thankful, but he is forewarned against requiring reciprocity as a condition of friendship. He is further told to pay little heed to ingratitude toward him. We can't dwell upon another's ingratitude without using up our time and talents unprofitably.

Because of the living Church, the interweaving of our lives occurs far more deeply and broadly. Because all of this interplay of lives is so vital, we need to be at our best for each other's sake. Life in the living Church is such that our priorities are always being probed and tested to see if we will place first things first.

When one is flying and nearing a busy airport, he assumes, hopes, and sometimes prays that the local air controllers will be doing their job well, and single-mindedly, so the plane can be guided safely down in the midst of many other planes. In one of the concourses at that same airport there may be a defective candy machine into which a frustrated air controller has put his coins to no avail. Clearly, the candy machine needs to be fixed, but any of us who have flown hope the frustrated controller will be at his best and at his station for our sake—and not banging on that vending machine.

Disciples are like the air controllers: we need to be at our best all of the time; we are always on duty; and people need us to be at our best in order to carry out our singular assignment of guiding and helping them. Our fellowmen can endure a careless delivery boy just as an airport can endure a broken vending machine, but the divinely sent disciple is crucial to the lives of others! The living Church helps us to keep our priorities straight, and there are in the living Church duties, reports, reminders, and personal prayers to keep us alert and at our posts; and conscience is a loyal companion.

Yet the gospel net gathereth of every kind. For instance, those who claim to care for the Church but who do not believe in it—the cultural Mormons—act as if the Church already belonged to history, and the Church embarrasses them, especially when it is so lively and living. Other members keep their devotions private instead of going public, for fear of being put out of the secular synagogue.

Still other members who may be critical of the living Church for being an authoritarian church are often also the very people who like an authoritarian government. Such citizens are sometimes possessed of what G. K. Chesterton, in his book *Robert Browning,* called a "disease of public spirit," a "drunkenness of responsibility" or a "wild desire to manage everything," feeling that unless they watch it, "the grass will not grow." Activity in the living Church would help these to focus on managing themselves better.

Much of what the living Church does consists of minding the Lord's flock and feeding his sheep in all their variety. The philosophies of the world, so lacking in their nutritional value, cannot be sufficient to fulfill the Savior's injunction, "Feed my sheep." We read that it is necessary, when we worship God, to "worship him in spirit and in truth." (John 4:24.) It is not enough simply to have the feelings; we must have the theological truths that permit us to understand God as he really is. And have them we do! The simple labor we have to perform is to read, ponder, and apply them; the searching required is a matter of searching pages of scriptures, not a desperate searching of the libraries of the world.

As we behave better, we actually learn more. (2 Peter 1:8.) When we keep his commandments, we also come to know of the doctrine whether it be of God or not, because truth testifies of itself. (John 7:17.) Learning more and behaving better are made easier in the fellowship of the living Church. So also in the family.

In the living Church it is vital that husbands and wives grow together in their gospel scholarship and in their Christian service. We do not want our men to be the theologians and our women the Christians. The living Church encourages symmetry, not separateness.

And as we learn and progress in the living Church, we come to personally know the truth, and the truth makes us free. (John 8:32.) As we "grow in grace and in knowledge of the truth" (D&C 54:40), we become more and more free—and less and less fettered by fables. All the fables did not end with Aesop, and modern myths abound.

A living disciple who learns a truth and applies it is reinforced by the consequences of those applications. His faith actually grows into knowledge. (Alma 32.) It is guided growth, for we have the promise from the Savior himself that God will guide us into all truth. (John 16:13.)

One reason the Church can stand with comparative independence is that it is founded upon *the truth* about things as they really are. Though the "way of truth shall be evil spoken of," and though such "pillars of the truth" are a temptation to some who want to try to pull them down, the living Church will stand. A dying civilization can, of course, be annoyed by the living Church. People who are cut to the very center by the truth, the laser of our Lord that emanates from the living Church, will gladly "turn away their ears from the truth, and be turned unto fables" (2 Timothy 4:4); it is so much less painful.

There are many people who wish to know some but not all of the truth. The Lord has said, "Behold, I say unto you, that they desire to know the truth in part, but not all, for they are not right before me and must needs repent." (D&C 49:2.) He has also said, "And your hearts are not satisfied. And ye obey not the truth, but have pleasure in righteousness." (D&C 56:15.) Sometimes we don't want to know all the truth because then we could not continue to have pleasure in unrighteousness, and the Lord will not suffer us "to take happiness in sin." (Mormon 2:13.) If we are double-minded, the straight and narrow way will be a special navigational challenge.

We cannot satisfy disparate hungers simultaneously, for the hungering for the praise of the world leads us away from hungering after righteousness. Jeremiah decried the tendency to conform to the world: "And they bend their tongues like their bow for lies: but they are not valiant for the truth upon the earth; for they proceed from evil to evil, and they know not me, saith the Lord." (Jeremiah 9:3.) A dying church would, institutionally, be incapable of indignation over certain wrongs; it could not be "valiant for the truth upon the earth." But the living Church with living prophets would speak out and be declarative on certain basic issues; it will not shrink from the pain of being on the point, for its Head saved us all by great pain.

The eventual growth of the Church prior to Christ's second coming was foreseen by the Lord: "But first let my army become very great, and let it be sanctified before me, that it may become fair as the sun, and clear as the moon, and that her banners may be terrible unto all nations." (D&C 105:31.) Presumably "very great" is something more than a church of a few million—

though, to be sure, validity, not numeracy, is the first test.

Of course, the growth of the Church will not occur in isolation from other events. Brigham Young foresaw in a revelation the following: "It was revealed to me in the commencement of this Church, that the Church would spread, prosper, grow and extend, and that in proportion to the spread of the Gospel among the nations of the earth, so would the power of Satan rise." (*Journal of Discourses* 13:280.) Thus the very growth and prosperity of the Church over which we rejoice will be accompanied, as the wheat is by tares, with a sobering and sweeping intensification of evil in the world!

The Twelve, not many months after the martyrdom of the Prophet Joseph Smith, issued a bold proclamation to the world in which they reminded us of still more sober events which lie ahead. ". . . As this work progresses in its onward course, and becomes more and more an object of political and religious interest and excitement, no king, ruler, or subject, no community or individual, will stand *neutral*. All will at length be influenced by one spirit or the other; and will take sides either for or against the kingdom of God. . . ." (*Messages of the First Presidency* 1:257.)

Thus when we speak of the living God, the living Church, living prophets, this produces a living religion that is difficult to disregard.

The living Church will have the capacity to do its part to fulfill the prophecies in the scriptures concerning the last days. The true Church will teach truths about things as they really were, as they really are, and as they really will be; therefore, it cannot possibly be fashionable in any age except a perfect age, and ours is not a perfect age.

The living Church will not be unmindful of political movements (righteous or unrighteous), but these will not be the focus of its activity and its energy any more than Jesus Christ was drawn off to use his perfect talents and energies in settling the disputes between Rome and the Jews anciently. There were surely wrongs to be remedied, but Jesus had more important things to do then and now.

So it is with the living Church today. It is obviously affected by, and cognizant of, political movements of one kind or another, but its mission is to declare the gospel of Jesus Christ and to perfect a people. Such basic institutional assignments cannot be set aside to take up some tactical concern, real or deserving though it is. The individual members of the living Church are urged to "be anxiously engaged in a good cause" and to do "many things of their own free will, and bring to pass much righteousness." (D&C 58:27.)

Such a stance may disappoint some who will want to enlist the Church's institutional aid in this or in that worthy project. There are many good causes in which people can be anxiously engaged "of their own free will." But the living Church, as an institution, must steer a course under the direction of the living God and his living prophets in order to render the maximum service to the human family through the preaching and the living of the gospel of Jesus Christ in its fullness. To let itself be diverted from that enormous task would be for the living Church to fail not only this generation but also future generations. Because his ends and purposes are "to bring to pass the immortality and eternal life of man," and because he has chosen to work (where we will let him) through us, to be diverted ourselves is to fail our friends and our families.

Of diversions, even good diversions, C. S. Lewis once observed wisely, "Every preference of a small good to a great, or a partial good to a total good, involves the loss of the small or partial good for which the sacrifice is made. . . . You can get second things only by putting first things first. . . ." (A Mind Awake, p. 60.)

Many of us miss the message implicit in the ranking of the first and second great commandments on which hang all the other commandments and laws. If, for instance, we do not learn to love the living God with all our heart, might, mind, and strength, then our might, mind, and strength are at best diverted to secondary tasks and, more likely, we will turn to tasks of which he would not fully approve. There are more people willing to do second, third, and fourth things; the first-things-first people are less numerous.

As for us, we can't have it both ways. We can't say to the Lord, "Thou art good and I worship thee and respect thy priorities, but, Lord, I have better things to do." Even if we serve him but do so slothfully, something is missing. Missed, too, is the personal growth that comes from goodness done gladly that would have increased our capacity for future service.

Personal integrity is vital in the living Church. We forget that Korihor actually believed but was possessed of a lying spirit. (Alma 30:42.) Agrippa believed the prophets, but when it mattered he lacked the courage to say so. (Acts 26:27.) How sad that so many cannot see that to be *put out* of the secular synagogues for one's belief in Christ is the first step toward being *let in* the kingdom of God! (John 9:22.) How ironic to see so many so-called free spirits imprisoning themselves in roles that, like Korihor's, cause them to be at cruel war with themselves. How lamentable that when all tongues will confess that Jesus is the Christ in that not-too-distant Judgment Day, there will be so many who were, in mortality, undeclared believers, who were actually persuaded and "almost" so acknowledged openly.

Mark it down, when one thinks he is being nice to God and "indulging" him by doing some of his work, that person is really indulging himself! A dying god, or an unnoticing god, might be so treated, but the living God will have none of it.

And thus it is, that the living God will not go away. He will continue to try to work with us, combining his perfect love and his omniscience in wonderful ways to bless us and to teach all who are willing.

So it is also with the living Church. It is not something we can attend to at Easter and Christmastime and feel as though we have done our duty and have been nice to the Church. The living Church will make the same kind of demands on us that the living God makes of us, although these demands and assignments are filtered, of course, through other imperfect people like ourselves. In the living Church, that good but unsophisticated elders quorum president, who does not know how busy and important we really are, has a way, happily, of showing up and calling us to the labor anyway. The living Church produces such living disciples!

The living God adjusts the tempo of his work in the living Church to suit the circumstances that, in his divine wisdom and as a loving Father, he knows need to be responded to.

The living God can give much operational revelation to the living Church just as he is doing in the true and living Church today. We read of how, during a strife-filled period of time around 12 B.C., leaders and some of their brethren "who knew concerning the true points of doctrine" were "having many revelations *daily*, therefore they did preach unto the people, insomuch that they did put an end to their strife in that same year." (Helaman 11:23. Italics added.) The quantity of revelations was obviously very great, though we do not at this point know much concerning their content, and they were sufficient unto the needs of their day.

Doctrinal revelation is more occasional, since the great foundation of the doctrine has been laid in the early days of this dispensation and before.

The Lord has spoken of the living Church's coming "forth out of obscurity." (D&C 1:30.) With the coming "forth out of obscurity," there are the stern challenges of visibility from which there can be no turning back. The Lord has also spoken of how the light of the gospel will "break forth." (D&C 45:28.) The imagery is not of a tiny soft beam of light such as we see coming furtively from under a closed door. Rather, breaking forth is more like a searchlight suddenly turned on whose light at first merely pierces the night sky, but soon fills it with the glow of the gospel. The living Church will be noticed, and this should put us as members on notice; we must be lighted, living disciples.

CHAPTER FOUR

THE REALITY OF THE LIVING PROPHETS

Surely the Lord God will do nothing, but he revealeth his secret unto his servants the prophets. (Amos 3:7.)

Terribly has His gospel suffered in the mouths of the wise and the prudent; how would it be faring now, had its first messages been committed to persons of repute, instead of those simple fishermen? (George MacDonald, *Life Essential*, p. 69.)

■Living prophets are the best source of understanding about living prophets. Next to honoring the Lord, they honor each other. The address of President Spencer W. Kimball in the April 1978 general conference is a source of further understanding about the challenges and responses of these unique men:

> Various excuses have been used over the centuries to dismiss these divine messengers. There have been denials because the prophet came from an obscure place. "Can there any good thing come out of Nazareth?" (John 1:46.) Jesus was also met with the question, "Is not this the carpenter's son?" (Matthew 13:55.) By one means or another, the swiftest method of rejection of the holy prophets is to find a pretext, however false or absurd, to dismiss the man so that his message could also be dismissed. . . . Perhaps they judged Paul by the timbre of his voice or by his style of speech, not the truths uttered by him.
>
> We wonder how often hearers first rejected the prophets because they despised them, and finally despised the prophets even more because they had rejected them. . . .
>
> The trouble with rejection because of personal familiarity with the prophets is that the prophets are always somebody's son or somebody's neighbor. They are chosen from among the people, not transported from another planet, dramatic as that would be!
>
> . . . the prophets have always been free from the evil of their times, free to be divine auditors who will still call fraud, fraud; embezzlement, embezzlement; and adultery, adultery. (*Ensign*, May 1978, pp. 76-77.)

In that same significant speech, President Kimball noted that prophets are sometimes wrongly perceived as being harsh and anxious to say to society, "I told you so." He then added his personal testimony: "Those prophets I have known are the most loving of men. It is because of their love and integrity that they cannot modify the Lord's message merely to make people feel comfortable. They are too kind to be so cruel. I am so grateful," he added, "that prophets do not crave popularity."

Those who crave popularity could not rouse a people to the basic realities of "things as they really are and . . . really will be." George MacDonald said it well: "It is not the hysterical alone for whom the great dash of cold water is good. All who dream life instead of living it, require some similar shock." (*George MacDonald Anthology*, p. 124.)

The prophets teach all of the gospel, but choose to emphasize those truths that are most relevant and most needed in the times in which they live. In an age, for instance, when the institution of the family was quite secure, prophets apparently felt less need to speak about that issue. Family life was given fact. But in our time, it has been necessary for prophets (particularly in the last part of this last dispensation) to remind all of society, as well as the saints, about the tremendous importance of the home. President Kimball did just that in that April 1978 conference when he said, "The home is the seedbed of saints" (*Ensign*, May 1978, p. 5), in a declaration that is scripture no less so than the comment of Paul to the saints in Corinth: ". . . my dearly beloved, flee from idolatry." (1 Corinthians 10:14.)

Comparatively, there are not many people in western civilization today who have a problem of idolatry in the sense of worshiping graven images, though they may idolize other wrong things. However, Paul faced a need to speak again and again about idolatry in a time when many homes were reasonably secure, while President Kimball has spoken again and again about the need for strengthening the home in a time when idolatry is not rampant.

In other dispensations, the truths given to us through modern prophets about a Heavenly Mother were not stressed, so far as surviving records show, but in this dispensation the Lord gave us this doctrinal truth through a prophet, Lorenzo Snow, whose sister, Eliza R. Snow, expressed it in her hymn "O My Father." Confirming the truths in that hymn, President Kimball has said: "Finally, when we sing that doctrinal hymn and anthem of affection, 'O My Father,' we get a sense of the ultimate in maternal modesty, of the restrained, queenly elegance of our Heavenly Mother, and knowing how profoundly our mortal mothers have shaped us here, do we suppose her influence on us as individuals to be less if we live so as to return there?" (*Ensign,* May 1978, p. 6.) Thus the basic truths are always the same, but the emphasis needed will be made by living prophets under inspiration from the living God, and the people of the living Church will respond.

No one appreciates the living scriptures more than living prophets. Yet even the living prophets have stressed the importance of having the Saints follow *living* oracles. Wilford Woodruff recalled a meeting in which the Prophet Joseph Smith turned to Brigham Young and said, "Brother Brigham, I want you to take the stand and tell us your views with regard to the written oracles and the written word of God."

In response to that invitation, Brother Brigham "took the Bible, and laid it down; he took the Book of Mormon, and laid it down; and he took the book of Doctrine and Covenants, and laid it down before him, and he said: 'There is the written word of God to us, concerning the work of God from the beginning of the world, almost, to our day. And now,' said he, 'when compared with the living oracles those books are nothing to me; those books do not convey the word of God direct to us now, as do the words of a Prophet or a man bearing the Holy Priesthood in our day and generation. I would rather have the living oracles than all the writings in the books.' "

At the end of these remarks the Prophet Joseph Smith said to the congregation: "Brother Brigham has told you the word of the Lord, and he has told you the truth." (*Conference Report*, October 1897, pp. 22-23.) Thus we see the tremendous importance of living prophets as well as the living word of God through the scriptures.

President Joseph Fielding Smith, a superb scripturalist, observed, "The First Presidency are the living oracles of God and the supreme adjudicators and interpreters of the law of the Church." (*Improvement Era*, 1966, p. 978.) Thus when we of the Church and the people of the world received a new revelation given in the spring of 1978, word of it came over the signatures of the First Presidency.

Individual revelations are as important as institutional revelations. President Smith went on to observe, "When Spirit speaks to spirit, the imprint upon the soul is far more difficult to erase. Every member of the Church should have impressions that Jesus is the Son of God indelibly pictured on his soul through the witness of the Holy Ghost." President Smith observed that such impressions on the soul that come from the Holy Ghost "are far more significant than a vision." (Ibid., p. 979.)

In this context, we can understand the great anxiety of President Brigham Young for each member of the Church to get his own witness that the work is true and not to rely overmuch upon the leaders of the Church for all spiritual impressions, especially such as those President Smith cited above. Of course, the reliance would be totally upon leaders of the Church for doctrinal pronouncements and for the policy guidance of the Church as a whole.

While still a member of the Council of the Twelve, President Kimball observed in a general conference of the speeches given by the Brethren, "Did you listen, or do you also build sepulchres for the dead prophets and tombs for those who have passed away long ago and disregard the living ones?" He went on to say, "I bear testimony also, in all solemnity, that this is the true and living Church and that it is officered by men who are called of God, and it is accepted of the Lord, and that the gospel which it promulgates, by these thousands of missionaries abroad and the other thousands here at home, is the gospel of Jesus Christ which will cure all ills and solve all problems and will exalt all mankind as well as save him." (*Conference Report*, October 1949, pp. 123-24.)

In August 1960 President Kimball wrote of the importance of Church members overcoming the tendency to regard yesterday's prophets more highly than today's prophets. He said, "Even in the Church many are prone to garnish the sepulchres of yesterday's prophets and mentally stone the living ones."

President Kimball then shared an important statement by President Woodruff about the changes in the expressions used by prophets to convey revelations. President Woodruff observed that the Prophet Joseph Smith often said " 'Thus saith the Lord' almost every day of his life in laying the foundation of this work. But those who followed him have not deemed it always necessary to say 'Thus saith the Lord'; yet they have led the people by the power of the Holy Ghost. . . . he is giving us revelation, and will give us revelation until this scene is wound up."

President Kimball cited the words of President Woodruff as a precise example of how there are revelations that are confirmed with new expressions:

"*I have had some revelations of late and very important ones to me . . .*"

"*Since I received that revelation . . .*"

"*The Lord showed me by vision and revelation . . .*"

"*He has told me exactly what to do . . .*"

"*. . . the God of heaven commanded me to do what I did do . . .*"

"*I went before the Lord and wrote what the Lord told me to write . . .*" (*Instructor*, August 1960, p. 257.)

Thus we see how different words are used in introducing, describing, or affirming revelation by different prophets. Expressions may change, but the process of revelation itself operates and is intact.

Those who are too concerned with phrasing will have difficulty following the prophet. President J. Reuben Clark, Jr., declared, "There are those who insist that unless the Prophet of the Lord declares, 'Thus saith the Lord,' the message may not be taken as a revelation. This is a false testing standard. For while many of our modern revelations as contained in the Doctrine and Covenants do contain those words, there are many that do not." (*Church News,* July 31, 1954, p. 10.)

Operational revelations come to living prophets to help them with individual situations even though the pronouncements resulting therefrom may not always have either general or doctrinal application. President Harold B. Lee spoke of an experience he had with a young serviceman in Korea to whom he extended a prophetic warning. After the young man had deeply impressed an audience with his testimony about chastity, President Lee was spiritually impressed to give the young man direct counsel: "Now, my boy, you have made a profound impression upon all of us. You have said that you would rather die than lose your virtue. But remember, the devil has heard you, as we heard you, and if I don't miss my guess, he is going to make you prove that you would give your life before you would lose your virtue. You had better be on guard." (*Ensign,* July 1972, pp. 102-3.)

President Lee's warning was relevant and helped to keep that individual on the proper path. Years later he met that same man, who was by then a grateful temple worker in the Los Angeles Temple. The prompting came at the crucial crossroads of that man's life.

How vital it is that each of us come to have a personal witness that we are led by living prophets. President Lee observed that someone once said, "That person is not truly converted until he sees the power of

God resting upon the leaders of this church, and until it goes down into his heart like fire." President Lee said this observation was "absolutely true," adding that "until the members of this church have that conviction that they are being led in the right way, and they have a conviction that these men of God are men who are inspired and have been properly appointed by the hand of God, they are not truly converted." (Ibid.)

In the living Church, members must have living testimonies of the living prophets as well as of the living scriptures and the living God. President Lee once gave a speech to seminary and institute faculty members on "The Place of the Living Prophet" in which he observed how proximity and familiarity sometimes get in the way of people's following the living prophet because "he is so close." He commented on the responsiveness of heaven to changing circumstances: ". . . had you ever thought that what was contrary to the order of heaven in 1840 might not be contrary to the order of heaven in 1960?" (Address to Seminary and Institute Faculty, Brigham Young University, July 8, 1968.)

If we believe in the living prophet, our faith will not die with a particular prophet but will be transferred to his successor. In that same important address, President Lee further quoted John Taylor as saying, "The principle of present revelation, then, is the very foundation of our religion." And of the books of scripture President Taylor said,

> Those books are good for example, precedent, and investigation, and for developing certain laws and principles. But they do not, they cannot, touch every case required to be adjudicated and set in order. We require a living tree—a living fountain—living intelligence, proceeding from the living priesthood in heaven, through the living priesthood on earth. . . .
>
> Adam's revelation did not instruct Noah to build his ark; nor did Noah's revelation tell Lot to forsake Sodom; nor did either of these speak of the departure of the children of Israel from Egypt. These all had revelations for themselves, and so had Isaiah, Jeremiah, Ezekiel, Jesus,

Peter, Paul, John, and Joseph. And so must we, or we shall make a shipwreck. (*The Gospel Kingdom*, p. 34.)

Thus we see how living prophets honor past prophets and at the same time defer to future living prophets.

Those who think of revelations merely as accommodations do not realize how much they reveal of themselves. When some are unable to accept a teaching before an amplifying revelation comes, and then are unable to accept the revelation—even though it was one they said they hoped for—the reasons reflect deepseated personal difficulties. What is so transparent (to everyone except them) is that they do not really want to bear the responsibility of believing in modern and continuing revelation, because of the demands this would make upon them. If they rejoice in one revelation, they affirm a process that may produce other revelations that, for them, would be hard to bear. By shifting their ground so unconsciously, they cut the very ground from under themselves. By advancing erroneous explanations of the process, they seek to shield themselves from responsibility.

Revelation is at one and the same time both a conservative force and a progressive force. It is conservative and stabilizing in that it places before us and affirms all that God has communicated to man in the past, giving us continuity. At the same time, the open-endedness of the process of revelation brings us truths and realities that are, to us, new.

When some initially are uneasy with the stand taken by the living prophet for and in behalf of the living God, this may mean that they are basically faithful but puzzled and simply need to work through the matter until they come to a feeling of peace and support. But some people are so frequently unsettled by what the living prophets say that it is likely they are unsettled in a more basic way.

Prophets have a way of saying what the people need to hear, not what they want to hear; and when people cannot accept these utterances, it is usually because they are uncertain at their very center about things as they really are. So often we find that in order to get to the heart of the matter, it is necessary first to get to the hearts of those involved. Prophets do that!

Following the living prophets is something that must be done in all seasons and circumstances. We must be like President Marion G. Romney, who humbly said, ". . . I have never hesitated to follow the counsel of the Authorities of the Church even though it crossed my social, professional, and political life." (*Conference Report,* April 1941, p. 123.) There are, or will be, moments when prophetic declarations collide with our pride or our seeming personal interests. It can happen in many ways: businessmen caught in Sunday-closing efforts who must decide how they really feel about the fourth commandment; theater owners showing near-pornographic films who must decide between prophets and profits; politicians involved in an erring movement that calls forth a First Presidency statement, forcing them to decide which flag to follow; academicians whose discipline gives rise to moral issues on which the Brethren speak out, who must choose between peers and prophets; laborers who are caught in union-shop and free-agency situations. For the participants, such painful episodes tend to force home the question: Do I believe in the living prophet even when he speaks on matters affecting me and my specialty directly? Or do I stop sustaining the prophet when his words fall in my territory? If the latter, the prophet is without honor in *our* country!

Our peer pressures, our economic interests, and our pride rest upon transitory things, and disciples must make decisions on the basis of things as they really are.

President Lee called ours a time of "sophistication . . . when there are many clever people who are not willing to listen to the humble prophets" because this takes courage. ("Sweet Are the Uses of Adversity," *Instructor,* June 1965, p. 217.) The poor who heard Isaiah denounce the princes for grinding "the faces of the poor" did not find those declarations difficult to accept. (Isaiah 3:15.) But the Lord said to the idle poor in this dispensation: "Thou shalt not be idle; for he that is idle shall not eat the bread nor wear the garments of the laborer." (D&C 42:42.)

Again the Lord warned: "Wo unto you rich men, that will not give your substance to the poor, for your riches will canker your souls; and this shall be your lamentation in the day of visitation, and of judgment, and of indignation: The harvest is past, the summer is ended, and my soul is not saved!" (D&C 56:17.)

A clear test of our readiness to hear the living prophets is our receptivity to the statements of the First Presidency. Of these President Ezra Taft Benson has said, "If we are living the gospel, we will feel in our hearts that the First Presidency of the Church not only have the right, but are also duty bound under heaven to give counsel on any subject which affects the temporal or spiritual welfare of the Latter-day Saints." (*Conference Report*, October 1950, p. 148.)

Being alive to the living prophets means, said President Romney, that "what the presidency say as a presidency is what the Lord would say if he were here, and it is scripture. It should be studied, understood, and followed, even as the revelations in the Doctrine and Covenants." (*Conference Report*, April 1945, p. 90.)

This is a hard but necessary dimension of the doctrine about living prophets, and each in his circumstantial turn will need to be tested to see if he really subscribes to it. Our relationship to living prophets is *not* one in which their sayings are a smorgasbord from which we may take only that which pleases us. We are to partake of all that is placed before us, including the spinach, and to leave a clean plate!

The solidness under extreme pressure that was shown by Shadrach, Meshach, and Abednego is what all of us need. Before they were thrown in the fiery furnace these men said humbly they didn't know whether God would rescue them or not, but they still wouldn't worship the false god, an indication of a settled soul. They knew God was there, that he was the living God, and that he would watch over them—even if they died. (Daniel 3:17-18.)

In keeping with what Wilford Woodruff and John Taylor said about the importance of living prophets, contemporary prophets give us important insights not unlike, and just as valid as, those we might find in the writings of Peter and Paul. Paul, for instance, drew upon the Greek Olympic games and linked it to pressing forward till we win the prize of life, an incorruptible crown. (1 Corinthians 9:24-26.) We see equally significant wisdom in words from the apostles of today. Elder Marvin J. Ashton has said, "We never give anybody a lift when we give them a free ride." There are times of tragedies in life when the best thing one can do, as Elder Boyd K. Packer has suggested, is to "pick up our handcart and head west."

Compare, for instance, Paul's counsel about forgetting that which is past (Philippians 3:13) or James writing on grudges (James 5:9) and Elder Packer's counsel in a general conference in which he spoke of a deep grievance that stood between certain individuals and how the parties had to finally learn to "leave it alone. Leave it alone." (Ensign, November 1977, p. 61.) We must not reopen past wounds or pick at the scabs of something that is healing.

Ponder likewise John's counsel about the lusts of the flesh (1 John 2:16-17) and Elder Delbert L. Stapley's statement, "Our great challenge is to learn how to control ourselves." (Ensign, November 1974, p. 21.)

Living prophets can select from our environment analogies that are especially appropriate to our time. Both Paul (1 Corinthians 3:2) and Elder Howard W. Hunter used a teaching analogy referring to milk, with the latter counseling, "It is not well for man to pray cream and live skim milk." (Ensign, November 1977, p. 54.)

Living prophets can reflect on the needs of today as did Old Testament prophets on the needs of ancient Israel. An Israel in captivity called for customized counsel, whereas modern prophets must respond and have responded to the perils of affluence among many Church members.

The living prophet will always be in touch with eternity and, in a sense, will therefore stand outside time as he reflects God's will to a people who may be too much caught up in the fashion or problems of any particular age.

The picture one gets of the dispensation of Noah is of a people who were increasingly wicked and who felt increasingly self-sufficient. Their attitude was described as follows: "And every man was lifted up in the imagination of the thoughts of his heart, being only evil continually." (Moses 8:22.) Their condition was described as follows: "The earth was corrupt before God, and it was filled with violence." (Moses 8:28-30. See also Genesis 6:5, 11, 13.)

It is chilling, therefore, to learn that the days preceding the second coming of the Savior will produce conditions parallel in many ways to those in the time of Noah. (Luke 17:26.) It will take living prophets to keep us from sliding into parallel insensitivity.

Evil people often think, as did Cain, that they are free. No doubt Noah's contemporaries regarded themselves as liberated and sophisticated. The perceptive columnist George F. Will observed of false freedom, "If you accept the modern notion that freedom is just the absence of restraints, then Hitler was a radically free man, a man operating on society from outside, unrestrained by any scruples or ties of affection." (*The Pursuit of Happiness and Other Sobering Thoughts*, p. 16.)

It is the living prophets who can tell us of true freedom as they bring to us a marvelous blend of objectivity and relevancy. The living prophets will not only have the living scriptures before them to provide a longitudinal look at human history, but also the needs and iniquities of their time. The living prophets will also have one other immense advantage besides the sweep of scriptural history: the far broader and deeper sweep of the Spirit, which can prompt prophets to say what needs to be said in a given day or decade.

The living prophets are not perfect men, but they live close to Him who is perfect. It is no real reflection on them that in their imperfections these great men at times wish to hold back or to hasten history. Peter smote off the ear of one of those who came to take Jesus captive on the Mount of Olives. (Matthew 26:51.) Peter did not understand that the "arrest" of Jesus should not be arrested, because the unfolding events would move from Gethsemane to Golgotha and then to an empty grave, all of which he would witness and preach about for years after.

When such great individuals move so marvelously along the straight and narrow path, it is unseemly of us to call attention to the fact that one of their shoelaces is untied as they make the journey.

These marvelous men often carry burdens that we as members of the living Church ought to carry and that we could carry if the Spirit were more often upon us. Moses said it best: ". . . would God that all the Lord's people were prophets, and that the Lord would put his spirit upon them." (Numbers 11:29.)

When these living prophets pass on, their labors do not end. The angel who appeared to John the Revelator told him, "I am thy fellowservant, and of thy brethren the prophets." (Revelation 22:9.)

When the Spirit teaches prophets the truth of things as they really are, this includes sensitizing these special men to the implications of what is just beginning, implications that are imperceptible to others. Prophets are alerted to tiny trends that bode ill for mankind. Prophets, therefore, are the Lord's early-warning system: they both detect and decry at his direction. What may seem to be a premature expression of prophetic concern is actually the early discovery of a difficulty that will later plague the people. Noah's neighbors would not listen to him, though there must have been an awful moment when they could see, too late, what was coming.

Prophets are, literally and figuratively, set apart from society so that they can better gauge impending problems, helping those people who will to either cease and desist from that which is wrong or to prepare for that which is about to be.

Accepting the counsel of living prophets requires of us an intrinsic obedience, rather than waiting for events to underscore the obvious. Humility can come to us through the compulsion of events, or we can be humble "because of the word." (Alma 32:14.) So it is with responding to the living prophets. We can be humble because of the words of living prophets, or we can engage in tardy and compelled acknowledgment of their accuracy. What is saved, of course, is not only time, but, more importantly, souls!

Decades ago, living prophets warned us, for instance, of the dangers of world Communism when many Americans saw it in our midst as nothing more than a series of harmless study groups. Years ago, living prophets warned us of the growing governmental paternalism at a time when many others rejoiced in bureaucratic benevolence and did not foresee how ominous that development was. Years ago when Americans were flushed with victory after a bloody World War II in which millions had died the world over, the living and gentle prophet, President George Albert Smith, said soberly that "unless we can call the people of this world to repent of their sins . . . the great war that has just passed will be an insignificant thing, as far as calamity is concerned, compared to that which is before us." (*Conference Report,* October 1946, p. 149.)

The world has been led to lazy stereotypes of prophets as being wild and fanatic people to be ignored. Such stereotyping is the work of him who has also encouraged art that portrays an effeminate Jesus. Lucifer just cannot bring himself to present things as they really are, for the truth is not in him.

Believers must not stereotype false prophets either, thereby failing to recognize them in their many forms. Just as the living prophets are consistent in their doctrines and objectives, so false prophets follow certain patterns. Peter warned us of false prophets who would "bring in damnable heresies, even denying the Lord that bought them." (2 Peter 2:1.) The denial of the divinity and the atonement of Christ is such a constant characteristic. We see it not only in the Sherems and Korihors of yesteryear but, today, among those leaders who espouse and promote a Christianity without a divine Christ. John the Beloved said, ". . . for the testimony of Jesus is the spirit of prophecy." (Revelation 19:10.) The living prophets will always testify of the reality and the livingness of Jesus Christ. Equivocators, prevaricators, and manipulators always fail this test.

Living prophets will likewise be concerned with telling us the truth and will not flatter us or give us the messages we want to hear. Jesus warned of false prophets who would come "in sheep's clothing, but inwardly they are ravening wolves." (Matthew 7:15.) The original Twelve were even counseled to be wary "when all men shall speak well of you . . . for so did their fathers to false prophets." (Luke 6:16.) The sharp call to repentance is always part of the profile of a true prophet.

When prophets speak "hard things against the wicked, according to the truth," the guilty "taketh the truth to be hard, for it cutteth them to the very center." (1 Nephi 16:2.) There is kindness in this pain, for as truth, the Lord's laser, cuts through to all but the hardest of hearts, so the healing light of the gospel is let in. The outer encrustations of evil can make us so insensitive that only the cuts "to the very center" have any hope of bringing the desired response!

Prophets not only call us to repentance for violating

existing gospel ground rules, but they also even give us further ground rules, for the "laws of the kingdom . . . are given by the prophets." (D&C 58:18.) False prophets, however, encourage slippage away from divine standards, as was the case in the sad demise of that special, happy culture in the Americas after the visit of the resurrected Jesus. False prophets lead the people "to do all manner of iniquity." (4 Nephi 1:34.)

Secular Sherems will arise *within* the flock, and there will come into our midst clever Korihors on whom the law can have no hold. (Alma 30:12.) Such will mock righteous traditions; they will say there is no Christ and, therefore, no atonement. They will promise their followers emancipation from such benighted beliefs, and will say that whatsoever people do is really no crime. They will ignore the signs in the universe that speak of the living God even as they demand other signs. They will also mock the real messengers of God, till there is no remedy except the coming of the judgments of God. (2 Chronicles 36:16.)

The elect will not be deceived. However, many others will be. (Matthew 24:11; Mark 13:22.) The elect who hear the living prophets will be blessed, for "he that receiveth a prophet in the name of the prophet shall receive a prophet's reward." (Matthew 10:41.) Since the rewards for bringing one soul to God include great joy "with him in the kingdom of my Father," how marvelous to contemplate one's joy with many such souls! (D&C 18:15.) Those who have stood forth and shone forth, the living prophets (and those who have received them), will, promised Daniel, "shine as the brightness of the firmament" and "they that turn many to righteousness as the stars for ever and ever." (Daniel 12:3.) Who, in the depths of his soul, would not want to share in this, the prophet's reward?

It is not enough, therefore, to define the living prophet as merely the current prophet who is alive today, though that is correct enough. The living prophets were all close enough to God (before they came here) to be chosen by him then, and they will be close to him in the eternities. Moreover, while their livingness includes such precious perpetuity, even in this fleeting frame of time called mortality, these men live with a richness and in a depth that desensitized sinners do not and cannot know. Indeed, it is precisely because the living prophets know and apply the truths about things as they really are and about things as they really will be that they can tell us so much about what really living really is!

CHAPTER FIVE

THE REALITY
OF THE
LIVING SCRIPTURES

Behold, the scriptures are before you; if ye will wrest them it shall be to your own destruction. (Alma 13:20.)

I am the same that leadeth men to all good; he that will not believe my words will not believe me—that I am. (Ether 4:12.)

■We must always remember that it was the very openness of the invitation from James, encouraging readers to ask for personal revelation, that struck deeply and with great force into the heart of young Joseph Smith. There were no living prophets to whom Joseph could go, and no living Church that he could then join. But there were living scriptures that urged him to approach the living God! Thus it was the living scriptures that set in motion events that would create the living Church and new living prophets.

We are encouraged to make the living scriptures relevant to our lives and to our times as did Nephi in his approach to gospel scholarship: "For I did liken all scriptures unto us, that it might be for our profit and learning." (1 Nephi 19:23.) Indeed, if we will do this, "feasting upon the word of Christ," and cultivate the ongoing gift of the Holy Ghost, who can give us the current "words of Christ," we can with "profit and learning" be shown "all things what ye should do." (2 Nephi 31:20; 32:3, 5.)

As to receiving inspiration to guide us individually, we are far more apt to have such divine guidance if we have first savored and pondered the written scriptures already available to us in the library of the Lord. How could one wish to meet the challenge of living without the living scriptures?

We are told through an inspired translation of Jesus' words that "the key of knowledge," which the Savior said had been lost or taken away is actually "the fulness of the scriptures." (Luke 11:53, Joseph Smith Translation.) How could one ever wish to cope with the challenges of learning without the "key of knowledge"?

The Prophet Joseph Smith once described the Book of Mormon as the "most correct" book available to man. (HC 4:461.) Would we want to make this mortal journey without that correct and precise guide?

How fitting it is that the second witness for Christ, the Book of Mormon, should come to us through one who loved so much the first witness of Christ, the Bible. The Prophet Joseph Smith said of the Bible, "[One] can also see God's handwriting in the sacred volume: And he who reads it oftenest will like it best." (HC 2:14.)

As a prophet, Joseph could understand things that are less clear to some of us. He said on one occasion, "The Book of Revelation is one of the plainest books God ever caused to be written." (HC 5:342.) This is like Nephi's delight in and praise of Isaiah. Many of the rest of us struggle through these two books.

To give one further indication of Joseph's biblical scholarship, he once observed that "Peter penned the most sublime language of any of the apostles." (HC 5:392.) In the midst of his great love for the Bible, the Prophet gave us these precautions, however: "There are many things in the Bible which do not, as they now stand, accord with the revelations of the Holy Ghost to me." (HC 5:425.) He explained, "I believe the Bible as it read when it came from the pen of the original writers. Ignorant translators, careless transcribers, or designing and corrupt priests have committed many errors." (HC 6:57.)

The Prophet also preferred the German translation of the Bible because it seemed to him to be "the most nearly correct translation" and the most in accord with the "revelations which God has given to me for the last fourteen years." (HC 6:307.) We see how vital modern revelation is in studying past revelations.

One of the striking findings for the student of the

scriptures is the frequency with which the same truth, the same idea, the same insight, the same concept appears (and often with exactly the same words) in various books of the scripture. This is true not only with major doctrines, but also with very minor things that witness to the fact that the doctrines and truths that reappear come from the same Source. No wonder the prophets are consistent with each other.

That they so abundantly agree with each other is no small point in attesting to the divinity of the various books of the scriptures. Where the prophets deal with the same subject, they are consistent. A computer would have been too clumsy, and prophets would have been too finite by themselves to have attempted such a marvelous matching. Of course, some prophets, particularly modern prophets, have added to the revelations of God—as is fitting in the dispensation of the *fulness* of time.

The scriptures form a seamless structure of truths, even though the truths were given in different places and different dispensations.

Paul counseled the Hebrew saints to "be content with such things as ye have." (Hebrews 13:5.) Notice how that admonition parallels Alma's counsel to himself when, on one occasion, he yearned mightily that he could have a greater impact upon the children of men, but concluded humbly, "I ought to be content with the things the Lord hath allotted unto me." (Alma 29:3.)

When the word *reality* is used the single time in all of scripture it refers to "that glorious day when justice shall be administered," and those who had earned it would be given "that happiness which is prepared for the saints." (2 Nephi 9:43-47.) The word *happiness* is used thirty times in the Book of Mormon. The plan of salvation is actually referred to as "the great plan of happiness." (Alma 42:8.) We are urged to read of this and other realities in the scriptures, for Alma described the "word of God, to which we owe all our happiness."

(Alma 44:5.) One wonders if anyone has ever put it more plainly than Samuel, the Lamanite prophet, who said of happiness to some of his contemporaries, "For ye have sought all the days of your lives for that which ye could not obtain; and ye have sought for happiness in doing iniquity." (Helaman 13:38.) Alma declared that "wickedness never was happiness." (Alma 41:10.) Another prophet, Mormon, observed that God will not suffer people to take happiness in sin. (Mormon 2:13.) Joseph Smith said that happiness is the object and design of human existence. (HC 5:134.)

Paul urged the saints in his day not to associate with those who were rude disbelievers. His conservative counsel sounds a little aloof until one remembers how much is at stake. C. S. Lewis in his "Reflections on the Psalms" says, "I am inclined to think a Christian would be wise to avoid, where he decently can, any meeting with people who are bullies, lascivious, cruel, dishonest, spiteful, and so forth. Not because we are 'too good' for them. In a sense because we are not good enough. We are not good enough to cope with all the temptations, nor clever enough to cope with all the problems, which an evening spent in such society produces. . . ." (*A Mind Awake*, pp. 160-61.)

Paul counseled the saints in Corinth "not to company with fornicators." (1 Corinthians 5:9.) He broadened the counsel to include not only fornicators but also "the covetous, or extortioners, or with idolators."

As President Harold B. Lee said, in order to help someone else "we must stand on higher ground" than he is standing on. We must be careful not to abandon that ground—for the sake of the sinner as well as for our own welfare. There is a difference between assisting the wounded Samaritan who needed help and companying with those who are evil.

In similar counsel given to the saints in Thessalonica, Paul said, "If any man obey not our word by this epistle, note that man, and have no company with him, that he may be ashamed. Yet *count him not as an enemy,* but admonish him as a brother." (2 Thessalonians 3: 14-15. Italics added.) In refusing to keep company with evil people, we do it not because they are our enemies, but because they are our friends. If we became just like them and did the things they do, we could not admonish them or help them "as a brother."

The same consistent pattern in the scriptures is available with key words like *trial* and *temptation.* The Lord in a revelation in 1834 spoke of his people as having been "brought thus far for a trial of their faith." (D&C 105:19.) He counsels us to "be patient in tribulation until I come." (D&C 54:10.) He said there will be great rewards in the kingdom of heaven for those who are "faithful in tribulation." (D&C 58:2.) He reminds us again that "after much tribulation come the blessings." (D&C 58:4.)

Just as the Lord counsels the Church to "stand independent" notwithstanding tribulation, so he also expects this of us as individuals. (D&C 78:14.) "And after their temptations, and much tribulation, behold, I, the Lord, will feel after them." (D&C 112:13.) Joseph Smith on one occasion said the Lord will have "a tried people." (HC 3:294.) The Lord said, "My people must be tried in all things." (D&C 136:31.)

Peter said to the saints, "Beloved, think it not strange concerning the fiery trial which is to try you, as though some strange thing happened unto you." (1 Peter 4:12.) Joseph Smith was counseled that his trials and tribulations would be for "a small moment" and that "all these things shall give thee experience, and shall be for thy good." (D&C 121:7; 122:7.) The excellent imagery given to us by Alma describes circumstances we may all come to know, at times, of "wading through much tribulation and anguish." (Alma 8:14.)

Peter likens the "trial of your faith" to the refining of gold. (1 Peter 1:7.) Jesus said that in the world we would have tribulation, but in him we would have peace, and in the midst of our tribulation we should be of good cheer because he had overcome the world. (John 16:33.)

We are told by Moroni in the book of Ether that we receive no witness until *after* the trial of our faith. (Ether 12:6.) But in all of this we can be assured that God will gauge the trial and tribulation and temptation so that there are (for the righteous and humble) either ways to escape or ways to cope. We are surely to pray that we will not allow ourselves to be led into temptation, and/or that we will be delivered therefrom. God is faithful and will not ask us to bear more than we can bear. (1 Corinthians 10:13.)

James reminded us that when someone is tempted he should not say, "I am tempted of God: . . . but every man is tempted, when he is drawn away of his own lusts, and enticed." (James 1:13-14.) So when we pray that we will not be led into temptation, we are praying for a capacity to control our own appetites.

We are to be extremely careful about temptation, but God has given us a guarantee that there will always be a way to escape, and/or that we will not be tempted above that which we are able to bear. This truth, echoed by different prophets in different dispensations, is vital to us; the very prophetic repetition is reassuring.

James says to us, "Blessed is the man that endureth temptation; for when he is tried, he shall receive the crown of life, which the Lord hath promised to them that love him." (James 1:12.)

God knows beforehand whether we can cope, but we need to know and to be able to have ultimate self-esteem by having overcome *before* added responsibilities and adventures come to us. God knows the outcome before the trial has begun, but we do not know, and so we must pass through certain experiences.

Mosiah describes patience as one of the virtues necessary for sainthood. (Mosiah 3:19.) Paul, in his epistles to the Romans, said that "tribulation worketh patience." (Romans 5:3.)

Three prophets use the same words, "past feeling."

Paul used them to describe how far gone some were in their lasciviousness. (Ephesians 4:19.) Even earlier, Nephi used them to sum up the imperviousness that is born of iniquity. (1 Nephi 17:45.) Moroni later described a totally decadent society as having reached the point when it was "past feeling." (Moroni 9:20.)

We see the words "love unfeigned" used by Paul (2 Corinthians 6:6) and by Peter (1 Peter 1:22). We also see the words "love unfeigned" in that grand revelation on priesthood authority given to the Prophet Joseph Smith. (D&C 121:41.)

Thus three prophets use those same two words—years and continents apart.

The Lord reminded us that our prayers will be granted if our lives are righteous and if we ask in faith for that which is expedient. (D&C 88:64-65, 78.) He attached the same condition in his visit to the Nephites when he said the prayers of the faithful will be granted if they ask for that "which is right." (3 Nephi 18:20.)

We are also given a vision of becoming sufficiently spiritual so that our very petitions are inspired beforehand (D&C 50:30), and thus they can be granted even as we ask (D&C 46:30).

The Lord has spoken of temptations "to prove thee, to know what was in thine heart." (Deuteronomy 8:2.) If we link that scripture up with one in Jeremiah in which the Lord says, "I the Lord search the heart, I try the reins, even to give every man according to his ways" (Jeremiah 11:20, 17:10), we see the ultimate expression of agency and divine justice. If each of us really finally receives that which has been really wanted, none could quarrel with the justice of God. Trials and tribulations tend to squeeze the artificiality out of us, leaving the essence of what we *really* are and clarifying what we *really* yearn for. Therefore, the record will be clear.

Paul said that "we must through much tribulation enter into the kingdom of God." (Acts 14:22.) "Every man's work shall be made manifest: for the day shall declare it, because it shall be revealed by fire; and the fire shall try every man's work of what sort it is." (1 Corinthians 3:13.)

In John we read: "Nevertheless among the chief rulers also many believed on him; but because of the Pharisees they did not confess him, lest they should be put out of the synagogue: For they loved the praise of men more than the praise of God." (John 12:42-43.) Our accepting things as they really are can result in others rejecting us, for there is surely the modern equivalent of being "put out of the synagogue" of secularism.

Agrippa, who almost was persuaded, is a later example of the power of peers. In Helaman we read of a group who had forgotten God in the very day that he had delivered them being chastized by a prophet who said their purposes were twofold: "to get gain, to be praised of men." (Helaman 7:20-21.) This linking of financial profit with praise of men shows up in the words of an earlier prophet, Nephi, who observed of priestcraft that it existed at all because men "preach and set themselves up for a light unto the world, that they may get gain and praise of the world; but they seek not the welfare of Zion." (2 Nephi 26:29.)

Just how fashionable it can be in some seasons to persecute the saints of God is seen in the words of Nephi when he says some of the churches of the world and some of the gentile nations that "slayeth the saints of God" actually do it "for the praise of the world . . . and bring them down into captivity." (1 Nephi 13:9.) Even today, those who turn against the Church do so to play to their own private gallery, but when, one day, the applause has died down and the cheering has stopped, they will face a smaller audience, the judgment bar of God.

We do not know all of the reasons in the episode involving Martin Harris, but in his correcting counsel, the Lord said, "And let him repent of his sins, for he seeketh the praise of the world." (D&C 58:39.) If we are not careful we too may be turned by the praise of the world and lose our humility and perspective rather than a manuscript.

Just how effectively the devil can mount a two-front war against us is seen in the words of the Lord wherein he speaks of "the fear of persecution and the cares of the world." (D&C 40:2.) If our appetites can be directed in such a way that we are caught up in the cares of the world, and if we are then also afraid of persecution because of doing what is right, we have been acted upon and are doubly deterred from discipleship. Some who might not fear persecution by itself do not choose to cope with the double load of persecution *plus* the cares of the world. Some for whom the cares of the world would not be sufficient to draw them away finally yield because of the fear of persecution.

Another dimension of this strain of similarities running through the scriptures can be seen in those scriptures that pertain to the weaknesses we have in life and how, though some are given to us of God to keep us humble, such defects can actually be a strength to us. The Lord assures us that "my grace is sufficient for all men that humble themselves before me." (Ether 12: 26-27.)

Paul speaks of his experiences with his thorn in the flesh and the Lord's counsel to him:

"And lest I should be exalted above measure through the abundance of the revelations, there was given to me a thorn in the flesh, the messenger of Satan to buffet me, lest I should be exalted above measure.

"For this thing I besought the Lord thrice, that it might depart from me.

"And he said unto me, My grace is sufficient for thee: for my strength is made perfect in weakness. Most gladly therefore will I rather glory in my infirmities, that the power of Christ may rest upon me." (2 Corinthians 12:7-9.)

We read from Book of Mormon prophets virtually the same words: "My grace is sufficient for the meek . . . [and] for all men." (Ether 12:26-27.) Moroni speaks the same truth. (Moroni 10:32.) Moroni also echoes John: both observed how "perfect love casteth out all fear."

(Moroni 8:16; 1 John 4:18.) We see many such similarities in the gospel truths given by different men at different times.

Finite men would be unable to deal with the rigid and multiple requirements of being thus consistent *unless* each prophet had been in personal contact with the Spirit of God. Clearly, the Prophet Joseph Smith, in translating the Book of Mormon and in recording the revelations in the Doctrine and Covenants, did not have time to consult a computer printout with various columns of concepts in order to select "one from column A and two from column B" so as to appear completely consistent with his predecessors. Rather, out the revelations flowed, carrying with them their own witnesses as to their truthfulness!

The Prophet was given a revelation describing the point to be reached when Satan is bound and time is no longer. (D&C 88:110.) Likewise John the Revelator said that when the seventh angel performs his task, "there should be time no longer." (Revelation 10:6.) Thus from John to Joseph the concept about the termination of time held constant.

With regard to trusting in the arm of flesh, the Old Testament contains a warning about trusting the arm of flesh instead of trusting in the Lord. (2 Chronicles 32:8.) Later in the Old Testament, Jeremiah complained of a circumstance in which some "trusteth in man, and maketh flesh his arm." (Jeremiah 17:5.) Paul warns against walking after the flesh instead of after the Spirit. (Romans 8:1.) Nephi says, "I will not put my trust in the arm of flesh." (2 Nephi 4:34.) Through the Prophet Joseph Smith, we are warned about not trusting in the arm of flesh. (D&C 1:19.) How constant that concept is. Regardless of the hemisphere or the time in which the prophet lived, this warning, too, stays the same.

We see this same prophetic parallelism in the words of the Savior, referring to the judgment day when of "every idle word . . . they shall give account thereof. (Matthew 12:36.) We read of a judgment time in which "our words . . . our works . . . our thoughts will also condemn us." (Alma 12:14.) We should combine these with the even more colorful description given by a Book of Mormon prophet who speaks of a judgment time when we will have "a perfect remembrance" and "a bright recollection" of our guilt. (Alma 5:18; 11:43.)

Surely there is more than coincidence to the similarities in the conclusion of a suffering Job who said, "I have *borne chastisement*, I will not offend any more" and the revelation given in modern times in which the Lord says to his disciples, "He that will not *bear chastisement* is not worthy." (Job 34:31 and D&C 136:31. Italics added).

Consider, for instance, the phrase "children of light," first used by the Lord (as reported by two of the Gospel writers, Luke and John) in a parable concerning the unjust steward. The Lord observed, "For the children of this world are in their generation wiser than the children of light" (Luke 16:8), suggesting an intense consistency within the wrong but demanding value system of the children of this world who act out their values in anything but a casual way. In a precious comment to his disciples, Jesus said, "While ye have light, believe in the light, that ye may be the children of light." (John 12:36.)

Writing years later, Paul took up the same theme when he said to the saints in Ephesus, "For ye were sometimes darkness, but now are ye light in the Lord: walk as children of light." (Ephesians 5:8.) Paul, in writing to the saints in Thessalonica, speaks synonymously of the saints as "children of the day" whom he urges to put on the breastplate of faith and love and the hope of salvation as a helmet. (1 Thessalonians 5:5.) King Benjamin speaks of those who have covenanted with Christ as "the children of Christ" whose hearts have been changed. (Mosiah 5:7.) About two thousand years later, in a revelation given in 1834 to Joseph Smith, the Lord used the same phrase, "children of light," making it synonymous with being prepared rather than being surprised. (D&C 106:5.)

As yet another example of this consistency, there are the various prophecies of events in the last days of the earth's history. Joel said, "The heavens and the earth shall shake." (Joel 3:16.) Haggai said, speaking for the Lord, "I will shake the heavens, and the earth, and the sea." (Haggai 2:6.) Isaiah, using somewhat different words, said, "The earth shall reel to and fro like a drunkard." (Isaiah 24:20.)

Centuries later, Paul, referring to that same day of judgment, said, speaking for the Lord, "I shake not the earth only, but also heaven." (Hebrews 12:26.) Still more centuries later, the Lord, speaking through the Prophet Joseph Smith of the last days, said, "The heavens shall shake and the earth shall tremble." (D&C 43:18.) Still later the Lord said, "I will not only shake the earth, but the starry heavens shall tremble." (D&C 84:118.)

As yet another dimension of the signs of the time, the Lord said, "The love of many shall wax cold." (Matthew 24:12.) We next hear that theme centuries later from the Lord himself, who said, "And the love of men shall wax cold" (D&C 45:27), which words were used in the Prophet Joseph Smith's translation of the 24th chapter of Matthew.

Consider, too, as a part of those engulfing and ending episodes the parallel accounts of the two prophets who will testify in Jerusalem in the last bloody and climactic days there. John speaks of two witnesses, duly appointed emissaries of the Lord and of his church, who will witness to the besieged city and then will be slain: "And their dead bodies shall lie in the street of the great city . . . three days and a half." (Revelation 11:8-9.) Joseph Smith identified these two individuals in a revelation given in 1832 as being "two prophets that are to be raised up to the Jewish nation in the last days, at the time of the restoration, and to prophesy to the Jews after they are gathered and have built the city of Jerusalem in the land of their fathers." (D&C 77:15.) Here we see once again the tight fit and perfect matching that carries on from prophet to prophet. Should we be surprised?

Placed alongside each other, the following interesting scriptures concerning learning tell us more together than separately.

Jesus said, "Learn of me . . . and ye shall find rest unto your souls." (Matthew 11:29.) A special kind of learning about particular truths comprehends the reality and existence of Jesus Christ as a resurrected Lord; it is the basis of all knowledge and must precede other forms of learning. Paul spoke of those who did not understand this central reality as being "ever learning, and never able to come to the knowledge of the truth." (2 Timothy 3:7.)

A hemisphere away and still earlier, Nephi was bemoaning the fact that men were foolish because "when they are learned they think they are wise, and they hearken not unto the counsel of God, for they set it aside, supposing they know of themselves, wherefore, their wisdom is foolishness." Nephi goes on to make it clear that "to be learned is good if they hearken unto the counsels of God." (2 Nephi 9:28-29.) But to be merely "puffed up because of their learning" is a very dangerous circumstance.

We read in the book of Jacob of a man named Sherem who is described as follows: "And he was learned, that he had a perfect knowledge of the language of the people; wherefore, he could use much flattery, and much power of speech, according to the power of the devil." (Jacob 7:4.) Sherem tried unsuccessfully to shake Jacob, a prophet who had received revelations from the Lord and who had seen angels. The temporarily saccharine Sherem even referred to the prophet as "Brother Jacob," and took the classic agnostic position: if there were a Christ, "I would not deny him; but I know there is no Christ, neither has been, nor ever will be." (Jacob 7:9.) Sherem was very scholarly and knew the scriptures, but the prophet Jacob said Sherem did not "understand them; for they truly testify of Christ."

Sherem, as did Korihor, confessed later on to having been "deceived by the power of the devil." Once more we see a conceptual consistency flowing through different prophets in different ages.

Notice the striking similarity between the words in Matthew, "Learn of me . . . and ye shall find rest unto your souls," and the words given centuries later, "learn of me . . . and you shall have peace in me." (Matthew 11:29; D&C 19:23.) The conceptual corridor is so consistent because it is part of the straight and narrow path; there is only one such path, and the Lord and all his prophets direct our thoughts and attention thereto.

It should not surprise us, then, to read of Jesus warning us about the possibility of mental adultery when a man "looketh on a woman to lust after her," only to find centuries later that same Lord saying that anyone who "looketh upon a woman to lust after her shall deny the faith." (Matthew 5:28; D&C 42:23.) Further, the Lord says that any persons who look on a woman to lust after her or if any shall commit adultery, "they shall not have the Spirit, but shall deny the faith *and shall fear*." (D&C 63:16. Italics added.)

This precision in recording events and attitudes exists even in the matters of seemingly the smallest detail. There is also consistency in the multiple references to a particular period of time, as we see in this next illustration by Elder Dean L. Larsen:

> From the first division among the children of Lehi, the righteous Nephites labored to convert their rebellious brethren, the Lamanites. As Jacob recorded, "Many means were devised to reclaim and restore the Lamanites to the knowledge of the truth; but it all was vain." (Jacob 7:24.)
>
> Enos added, "And I bear record that the people of Nephi did seek diligently to restore the Lamanites unto the true faith in God. But our labors were vain." (Enos 1:20.) A long history of such experiences—not to mention many savage wars between the two groups—made the Nephites skeptical of attempts to preach to the Lamanites, and when the sons of Mosiah planned their mission "our brethren . . . laughed us to scorn." (Alma 26:23.) . . .
>
> Many years later, as Moroni looked back on the

remarkable achievements of those missionaries, he accurately pinpointed the cause of their success: "Behold, it was the *faith* of Ammon and his brethren which wrought so great a miracle among the Lamanites." (Ether 12:15. Italics added.) Mormon made almost the same observation about the missionary labors of Nephi and Lehi, the sons of Helaman, who followed the sons of Mosiah on the same missionary trail and succeeded in converting virtually the entire Lamanite nation. (See Helaman 5:50-52.) He said, "Behold, it was the faith of Nephi and Lehi that wrought the change upon the Lamanites." (Ether 12:14.) (Dean L. Larsen, "Prayer: The Missionary Tool in Everyone's Hands," *Ensign*, October 1977, p. 38.)

Paul, in writing to the saints in Corinth, reminded them that the temptations they had were common to man and to life. He then went on to assure them that God would not suffer them to be tempted above that which they were able to bear but would always make with the temptation a way to escape it so that it could be borne. (1 Corinthians 10:13.) Alma, a hemisphere away and over a century earlier, urged the people to pray "that ye may not be tempted above that which ye can bear." (Alma 13:28.) The same words Paul used were used by the Lord centuries later when he said, "And again, I say unto you, that my servant Isaac Morley may not be tempted above that which he is able to bear." (D&C 64:20.) A divine Father measures out our growth experiences according to our readiness and capacity to cope. Peter, writing in his second epistle, reassured all who would heed that "the Lord knoweth how to *deliver* the godly out of temptations." (2 Peter 2:9. Italics added.) The practical counsel of James must always be heeded too: "Let no man say when he is tempted, I am tempted of God: for God cannot be tempted with evil, neither tempteth he any man." (James 1:13.)

Obviously the prophets and apostles of different dispensations have written or spoken on these truths without consulting with each other to correlate what they were saying. They were correlated by that powerful and perfect correlator, the Holy Ghost.

We see this same interior consistency as the prophets of God assure us that we will not be tested with trials and tribulations beyond that which we can handle in life if we are righteous and prayerful. Hundreds of years after the instructions from Alma, Peter, and Paul, the Lord, in a revelation given in 1831, said to his modern disciples, "Behold, ye are little children and ye cannot bear all things now; ye must grow in grace and in the knowledge of the truth." (D&C 50:40.)

This prophetic parallelism continues with precision even in word detail. We find, for instance, James counseling us with regard to prayer, saying, "Ye ask, and receive not, because ye ask amiss." (James 4:3.) The prophet Nephi took note of that same condition and said, "My God will give me, if I ask not amiss." (2 Nephi 4:35.)

The Lord says, "Men ought always to pray, and not to faint." (Luke 18:1.) Centuries later the same Lord said, "Pray always, that ye may not faint, until I come." (D&C 88:126.)

Lest too much be made of this parallelism, revelations given without the difficulties of transmission and translation, such as were experienced in bringing the Bible forth, often give us added information. "Ask, and it shall be given you." (Matthew 7:7.) "And whatsoever ye shall ask the Father in my name, which is right, believing that ye shall receive, behold it shall be given unto you." (3 Nephi 18:20.)

Notice the refinement and elaboration that occurs in Paul's warning words to Timothy about those who supposed that "gain is godliness." (1 Timothy 6:5.) Paul worried about those who are rich falling into temptations and snares, "For the love of money is the root of all evil." (1 Timothy 6:10.) The Book of Mormon adds to our understanding of the role of wealth: "And *after* ye have obtained a hope in Christ ye shall obtain riches, if ye seek them; and ye will *seek them for the intent to do good*—to clothe the naked, and to feed the hungry, and to liberate the captive, and administer relief to the sick and the afflicted." (Jacob 2:19. Italics added.)

Notice the connecting tendons of tenderness when Paul spoke of the need to speak "the truth in love" (Ephesians 4:15) and urged that we should confirm our love toward one who stands disciplined and reproved lest he "be swallowed up with overmuch sorrow" (2 Corinthians 2:7). In the latter days, the Lord has counseled us to reprove as moved upon by the Holy Ghost, and even then we are to show forth afterwards an increase in our love toward him who has been reproved "lest he esteem thee to be his enemy." (D&C 121:43.)

Peter, in tribute to the Master, noted how Jesus was reviled but "when he was reviled, reviled not again." (1 Peter 2:23.) Alma's counsel to us is: "Do not revile against those who do cast you out." (Alma 34:40.) We are told even to avoid reviling against revilers. (D&C 19:30.) And again, "revile not against those that revile." (D&C 31:9.)

Just as we are told by a prophet that the Book of Mormon "shall establish the truth" of the Bible, which includes the acts of the Twelve Apostles of the Lamb, so indeed do all scriptures establish the truth of one another. (1 Nephi 13:40.)

The scriptures are cohesive, correlated, and crucial because, as the Lord himself said, "These words are not of men nor of man, but of me." (D&C 18:34.) The chief carrier of this role of convincing people about the divinity of Jesus Christ is the Book of Mormon, which the Lord said would prove "to the world that the holy scriptures are true, and that God does inspire men and call them to his holy work in this age and generation, as well as in generations of old; Thereby showing that he is the same God yesterday, today, and forever. Amen." (D&C 20:11-12.)

Paul, in his writings to Timothy, spoke of those who have "erred from the faith, and *pierced* themselves through with many sorrows." (1 Timothy 6:10. Italics added.) Jacob, in the Book of Mormon, speaks of those victimized by unchastity who "instead of feasting upon the pleasing word of God have daggers placed to *pierce* their souls and wound their delicate minds." (Jacob 2:9. Italics added.) In this time of gross unchastity Jacob describes many as having reached a condition wherein "many hearts died, *pierced* with deep wounds." (Jacob 2:35. Italics added.)

Note how Paul seeks to define "godly sorrow" as working real repentance to salvation. (2 Corinthians 7:10.) How parallel that is to the unique but similar concept of "the sorrowing of the damned" spoken by Mormon in which he distinguishes between the discomforting sorrow of the world and real sorrow. (Mormon 2:13.)

One sees poignant parallels in Paul's description of his discipleship—"I *press toward* the mark for the prize of the high calling" (Philippians 3:14; italics added)— and Nephi's description of what disciples must do to remain in the straight and narrow path: "Ye must *press forward* with a steadfastness in Christ" (2 Nephi 31:20; italics added). Discipleship is not simply surviving and enduring; discipleship is a pressing forward, a creative Christianity. Discipleship does not wait to be acted upon, but instead acts upon men and circumstances to make things better.

It is not simply the general parallels we see among the utterances of the prophets of different dispensations, but the precision in these parallels. Of course, more divine data has been given to some prophets than others, but the "bottom line" is not the comparative candlepower given to each of the Lord's prophets; rather, it is how, each time the light of heaven is focused, it shines upon the same basic truths!

A forger would not err by having Lincoln's face on a twenty-dollar bill. His mistakes would occur in smaller things where errors in details would give him away. Thus it is so validating to see the interior consistency of the scriptures in so many small or less heralded things.

For the indifferent reader of the scriptures, and certainly for the disbeliever, the conceptual and phrasing parallels noted in this chapter will be unpersuasive. These parallels are cited for the believer, for he will understand how the gospel, whether given anciently or modernly, reflects the same Source. He will appreciate why the truths, and sometimes even the words, hold constant from age to age.

It is a reflection of the inspiration of Joseph Smith, not his acumen, that he did not need to remember (along with hundreds of other concepts and words) where, for instance, he had seen the phrase "past feeling" in the writings of Paul; the phrase was there in the words of Nephi and Moroni, waiting to be translated.

For the language, truths, and concepts in different dispensations to fall back into place should not surprise those of us who see the gospel as the reality of things as they really were, as they really are, and as they really will be. Joseph Smith and his prophet colleagues did not simply *"guess right,* among so many" such examples—but were *guided right* by God. (Helaman 16:16. Italics added.)

God, who does not grow weary of making all daisies alike and whose course is one eternal round, does not tire of certain truths as do we mortals. Nor does the repetition of a true phrase reduce its relevancy; it vouches for its validity.

With regard to the simplicity of the living gospel, Paul expressed concern in his second epistle to the saints at Corinth lest their "minds should be corrupted from the simplicity that is in Christ." (2 Corinthians 11:3.)

As the author has expressed this thought on another occasion, we like intellectual embroidery. We like complexity because it gives us an excuse for failure, that is, as you increase the complexity of a belief system, you provide more and more refuges for those who don't want to comply; you thereby increase the number of excuses that people can make for failure to comply, and you create a sophisticated intellectual structure which causes people to talk about the gospel instead of doing it. But the gospel of Jesus Christ is not complex. It strips us of any basic excuse for noncompliance, and yet many of us are forever trying to make it more complex. ("The Simplicity of the Gospel," BYU Speeches of the Year, May 4, 1969, p. 6.)

Paul observed that we shouldn't be surprised if Satan's ministers also be "transformed as the ministers of righteousness" (2 Corinthians 11:14-15) who in their pseudosophistication exalted themselves "against the knowledge of God" (2 Corinthians 10:5). They felt self-sufficient and were impervious to the insights that came to them from the living God or his living prophets. When evil encrusts itself with a self-justifying system of thought and artificial values, this shuts out the light of the gospel. Thus we see why Paul was anxious about the corrupting influence of complexity.

President Joseph F. Smith said, "God, in his revelation to man, has made his words so simple that the humblest of men, without special training, may enjoy great faith, comprehend the teachings of the gospel, and enjoy undisturbed their religious convictions." (Gospel Doctrine, p. 9.)

There is another very significant reality about the simplicity of the gospel way that, especially in this age, we will come to appreciate much more. That reality is this: Once individuals or nations depart from divine standards and get off the straight and narrow way, they find on either side of that rigorous path terrible thickets. Things get very confused and incredibly complicated. When we get off the course, it becomes very difficult to chart any consistent course at all. The way we solve one problem merely creates another that is sometimes worse. Compensating turns in these mazelike thickets are impossible.

No wonder in such situations the wisdom of man perishes and men's hearts fail them. So stranded, many people plead, "Save us from ourselves," and in a disbelieving time the plea is not made to God but to government.

For instance, if people get off the straight and narrow way concerning the essentiality of the family institution, they will find that all the substitute programs and compensatory institutions will finally fail, and they will wonder why. If people get off the straight and narrow way concerning the absolute standards of chastity and fidelity, notice how hard it is for such individuals to decide when relative infidelity is acceptable. They then involve themselves in tortured choices and rationalization, which would be amusing if it were not so tragic. So it goes. On each side of the straight and narrow way are complexity and uncertainty on a scale that exceeds man's ability to cope. Once we leave the straight and narrow way, nothing will ever be simple again.

Far from admiring those who have thrown themselves into these thickets for their heroic efforts to cut their way clear, we should seek to rescue them from their foolishness. For them, the only way forward is back!

The Lord described himself as having "sent forth the fulness of his gospel, his everlasting covenant, reasoning in plainness and simplicity." (D&C 133:57.) It is the gospel to be "proclaimed by the weak and the simple" (D&C 1:23)—weak, at least, as the world measures weakness, and simple as the world measures simpleness. (1 Corinthians 1:19-27.) Yet as Alma observed, "By small and simple things are great things brought to pass; and small means in many instances doth confound the wise." (Alma 37:6.)

People are being deflected by simplicity in our day, but this is not the first time. It happened in Moses' day in a very graphic demonstration of this basic need for simple faith and trust in the living God and the living prophet. There were those then who, "because of the simpleness of the way, or the easiness of it," perished physically because they could not perform one simple act that they had to perform: to look upon the brazen serpent and be healed of the bites they had received from the fiery flying serpents. (1 Nephi 17:41.) Parallel information, less, but still enough, is given us concerning the episode in the Old Testament. (Numbers 21:6-9.)

Paul, in writing to the saints in Rome, said that he wished them to be "wise unto that which is good, and *simple* concerning evil." (Romans 16:19. Italics added.) In a second epistle to the Corinthians, Paul rejoiced in the fact that he had shared the testimony of his conscience "in simplicity and godly sincerity, not with fleshly wisdom." (2 Corinthians 1:12.) In his previous epistle to the saints at Corinth, he indicated that he had preached the word of God "not in the words which man's wisdom teacheth, but which the Holy Ghost teacheth." (1 Corinthians 2:13.) This scripture can be compared with the words of Jacob, who said, ". . . for the Spirit speaketh the truth and lieth not. Wherefore, it speaketh of things as they really are, and of things as they really will be; wherefore, these things are manifested unto us plainly, for the salvation of our souls." (Jacob 4:13.) It is vital that we be "simple concerning evil"—"for the salvation of our souls."

Surely anything as powerful and important as the gospel message ought to be given to us in simplicity and plainness, so that we are not kept from the truth because we do not know how to understand it. G.K. Chesterton wrote these relevant lines of poetry:

> Step softly, under snow or rain,
> To find the place where men can pray;
> The way is all so very plain
> That we may lose the way.
> —"The Wise Man"

On one occasion in Jerusalem when Jesus walked in the temple in Solomon's porch, people gathered around him and said to him, "How long dost thou make us to doubt? If thou be the Christ, tell us plainly. Jesus answered them, I told you, and ye believed not: the works that I do in my Father's name, they bear witness of me. But ye believe not, because ye are not of my sheep, as I said unto you. My sheep hear my voice, and I know them, and they follow me." (John 10:22-27.) That searing indictment was very plain and is echoed by this statement in modern revelation: "And ye are called to bring to pass the gathering of mine elect; for mine elect hear my voice and harden not their hearts." (D&C 29:7.) This very trenchant truth about who will hear and who will not hear reflects, of course, another sobering but simple reality in the gospel.

We may think that we can handle plain speaking better than we really can. Such was the case with Jesus' disciples in the Holy Land as he approached the end of his ministry. We read that "his disciples said unto him, Lo, now speakest thou plainly, and speakest no proverb. Now are we sure that thou knowest all things, and needest not that any man should ask thee: by this we believe that thou camest forth from God. Jesus answered them, Do ye now believe? Behold, the hour cometh, yea, is now come, that ye shall be scattered, every man to his own, and shall leave me alone: and yet I am not alone, because the Father is with me." (John 16:29-32.) Little did the several disciples realize how, when they decided to "go a fishing" after Jesus' crucifixion, they would soon see the resurrected Jesus and know him not. (John 21:3.)

We should be grateful for all the plainness and simplicity that God has given to us, for he measures and apportions to us as we are ready. When we are possessed of great truths or insights it is important that we speak plainly. Paul said as much: "Seeing then that we have such hope, we use great plainness of speech." (2 Corinthians 3:12.)

Of the loss of certain parts of the scripture it is significant that one prophet said that "many parts which are plain and most precious" are missing. (1 Nephi 13:26.) The equating of plainness and preciousness is significant. If we are not careful, God can take away his plainness from us, and we can come in our pseudo-sophistication to despise the words of plainness. (Jacob 4:14.)

We have been given so many answers in the scriptures that, as someone observed, we could compile "Gospel Questions for Gospel Answers." We have actually been given far more answers than we have posed good questions.

The advantages flowing from scholarship in the scriptures include not only the truthful content and the useful insights to be gleaned and that can be brought to bear on problems of today (personal or institutional), but also the reality that the very reading of the scriptures puts us in touch with what God said to others in other days. It thereby creates an atmosphere into which new inspiration can come, if needed.

It is all very much like a composer's being sufficiently inspired by hearing great music to create additional great music. An artist may stumble upon a scene of great beauty that sparks in his mind a painting that has never before been on canvas. Previous revelations in the scriptures are like the "clean sea breeze of the centuries" that can be played by us, putting things in a perspective as they really are—much as a person with a few aches and pains can, by visiting a hospital, put his own physical problems in fresh and grateful perspective.

As always there must be balance. The inordinate reading of the living scriptures that crowded out one's family, one's neighbors, and Christian service would be an error. One could become monastic though scholastic.

Christian service to mankind could crowd out the living scriptures and become so consuming that one could forget his duties to family and to God, being a do-gooder almost as an escape from the family framework.

On the straight and narrow way, we must always keep our balance. The gospel gives us a center of gravity that keeps us from being tipped or tossed from side to side.

Detractors may argue, wouldn't it be better for one to be righteous, even though monastic, than to be a troublemaker? The answer would be yes only if those two choices were our only choices. It might also be advanced that it would be better to have someone engaged in great service to the community, even if he did not worship God, than to be a hypocritical worshiper of God while doing nothing to help his community. But again, those are not the only two choices.

The point is that symmetry in our spiritual makeup gives us a chance to strike the balance that can give us maximum happiness and permit us to be of maximum service to others. Along the pathway set forth by Jesus of Nazareth, one of the great aids to balance is the regular reading of the living scriptures.

Because the scriptures do come to us through mortals, some half-believers fret unduly over details and look beyond the mark. Would we have wanted Joseph Smith to write, at age fourteen, his account of the First Vision? That he did as he was instructed in that great theophany was the most important and immediate thing required of him. What he wrote years later of that vision is so much richer, more revealing, and more powerful than it would have been in that spring of 1820. At that time he was inspired, directed, and instructed. His written reflections and recording were to come later—much as was the case with Nephi when he wrote later of some of the experiences through which he had earlier passed—and so much more tellingly and wisely!

Paul felt the love of God on the road to Tarsus, but, happily, he waited until later to write his superb treatise on love in his epistle to the Corinthians. (1 Corinthians 13.)

The Lord's sincerity is one of the reasons he has given us living scriptures in plainness, simplicity, and sincerity. People multiply words for many reasons, and one of the reasons is insincerity. As George Orwell has said, "The great enemy of clear language is insincerity. When there is a gap between one's real and one's declared aims, one turns, as it were instinctively, to long words and exhausted idioms, like a cuttlefish squirting out ink." (Quoted in John R. Trimble, *Writing with Style*, p. 3.) Insincerity is why it is impossible for some people to "get to the point." They circle an issue because, not being settled within their own soul, they cannot come to rest.

There is a lack of straightforwardness in the secular world for still other reasons. People may be showing off and playing to the galleries in their use of words, hoping to impress others. Some want to appear mysterious; wishing to be looked up to, they use language to put others down, producing distance between themselves and others rather than bringing themselves closer to others. Others get snared in the webbing of their own semantics and cannot free themselves even though they might wish to. And some want to hide within their verbiage so their true feelings are *not* made known.

There is such a difference between waffling and witnessing!

Winston Churchill said of military secrets that in wartime it is necessary for the truth to be surrounded by a bodyguard of lies. But gospel truths must always be "fair as the sun, clear as the moon," being set forth plainly, straightforwardly, and simply. There is too much chance of miscommunication and too much risk of having someone deflected from discipleship because of misunderstanding. To give a tourist wrong directions is inconvenient, but to misdirect an individual's life is intolerable.

Given the impenetrability of the human heart on occasions, the words of the Lord must be pointed enough to cut into the heart and to stir our soul. Dull words, or words that simply circle the subject, will not do it. True principles must be piercing enough to penetrate the heart and the mind so that the communication is "on the record." John the Baptist's simple eleven-word denunciation of Herod was resented but could not have been misunderstood: "It is not lawful for thee to have thy brother's wife." (Mark 6:18.)

Does anyone think that on that occasion when Jesus sent a message to Herod, through some Pharisees who were to go back to Herod "and tell that fox," the message went undelivered? (Luke 13:32.) The language of diplomacy has its purposes, but they are not universal.

Finally, when Paul speaks of our being compassed about with a "cloud of witnesses" (Hebrews 12:1), it is more than lovely imagery. The serious reading of the scriptures really does give us the feeling of being attended to and even of being gathered in. As we are enveloped in the experiences and the expressions of past notables, we can almost hear them talking. Their presence is a friendly presence and one of encouragement. By listening to their words, we will understand that history is more than the "strange, mournful mutter of the battlefield."

The disciple, through the living scriptures, hears the strains of immortal music played by prophets, a symphony of seers. The notes struck are often the same, but, like the opening bars of Beethoven's Fifth Symphony (which were used by allied radios in World War II to contact friends in enemy territory) we do not mind if the same scriptural notes are struck in order to get our attention, to instruct us and to touch us, because we do live in a world that is "enemy territory."

CHAPTER SIX

THINGS AS THEY REALLY WILL BE

For our words will condemn us, yea, all our works will condemn us; we shall not be found spotless; and our thoughts will also condemn us; and in this awful state we shall not dare to look up to our God; and we would fain be glad if we could command the rocks and the mountains to fall upon us to hide us from his presence.

But this cannot be; we must come forth and stand before him in his glory, and in his power, and in his might, majesty, and dominion, and acknowledge to our everlasting shame that all his judgments are just; that he is just in all his works, and that he is merciful unto the children of men, and that he has all power to save every man that believeth on his name and bringeth forth fruit meet for repentance. (Alma 12:14-15.)

■The judgment day is one of the things that really will be. The "future shock" of that judgment and the events to precede it will be without parallel. The dramatic day described so powerfully by Alma will be a highly compressed and collective moment of truth. This will be the day when every knee shall bow and every tongue confess Jesus is the Christ. (Philippians 2:10-11.) No mortals will be standing that day. Those who were cruelly used by the adversary will see that awful reality. Nephi said the unrepentant guilty would "remember [their] awful guilt in perfectness, and be constrained to exclaim: Holy, holy are thy judgments, O Lord God Almighty—but I know my guilt; I transgressed thy law, and my transgressions are mine; and the devil hath obtained me, that I am a prey to his awful misery." (2 Nephi 9:46.) Jesus, who purchased us and who owns us, will require this owning up. They who transgressed divine law will openly admit that their transgressions are their own and cannot be laid at someone else's door.

In writing of this event that really will be, the apostle John described how "the kings of the earth, and the great men, and the rich men, and the chief captains, and the mighty men . . . hid themselves in the dens and in the rocks of the mountains; And said to the mountains and rocks, Fall on us, and hide us from the face of him that sitteth on the throne, and from the wrath of the Lamb." (Revelation 6:15-16.) This is high drama. This is a final confrontation with the ultimate reality, the living God.

On that dramatic day there can be no saving swagger—no panache. On that day there can be no grievance with God that can be advanced at all. In that scene described by John and Alma, those whose grievance with God and his gospel was that his gospel was too plain and too simple will be simply speechless.

The living scriptures will have been before us. Living prophets' words will have previously penetrated *every* culture and *every* clime. Goethe said that "architecture is frozen music," and the scriptures are the preserved moral music of the universe that God kept repeating for mankind over the centuries.

The promised day of judgment will come, and all men will be left "without excuse." (D&C 101:93; Romans 1:20.) All individuals will receive "according to their works, according to the desire of their hearts." (JS-V 1:9.) The justice and mercy of God will have combined so that by then all inhabitants of the earth will have heard the gospel of Jesus Christ sufficiently to be fully accountable for it. Even those who died without that opportunity will by then have heard the gospel "that they might be judged according to men in the flesh, but live according to God in the spirit." (JFS-V 1:34, 59.) What President Joseph F. Smith saw was just what Peter saw much earlier when he wrote of the preaching of the gospel "to them that are dead, that they might be judged according to men in the flesh, but live according to God in the spirit." (1 Peter 4:6.)

All will have heard from living prophets (through preaching and through the scriptures), so that personal accountability will be just as complete as Nephi indicated: "And you that will not partake of the goodness of God, and respect the words of the Jews, and also my words, and the words which shall proceed forth out of the mouth of the Lamb of God, behold, I bid you an everlasting farewell, for these words shall condemn you at the last day." (2 Nephi 33:14.)

Each individual will have had full opportunity to forge his decision, to give his real desires full expression. We will receive what we really chose, and none can or will question the justice or mercy of God.

Those who regarded the scriptures as overdrawn in the description of the contest between evil and righteousness on this earth will not smugly so maintain at that day, for they will see why the earnest words of various prophets were really needed, such as the words of President Charles W. Penrose: "This is a real warfare that is taking place on this planet where you and I live." (*Conference Report*, October 1906, p. 54.)

Those wreckers who wrongly behaved as if freedom were the absence of any restraint and who knocked down supposed barriers only to be imprisoned within their own rubble will then see clearly things as they really are. And those who threw themselves, time and again, against the rock of revelation will understand why they and the gates of hell could not prevail against it. The pride of the world will fall, and great will be the fall thereof. Those will see their folly who resisted the truth by saying and feeling:

"Can anything so simple be true?"

"What will others think of me if I believe?"

"What will happen to my heavy investment in doubt and in a worldly life-style?"

"Why does the Lord demand so much of us by insisting that we walk by faith?"

These who have stood at the door of discipleship will be shown to have been too proud to enter, for they will have let their pride stroke their doubts and caress their excuses.

In that same glorious day we will see how all great

and true principles cut two ways into time—forward and backward. A grand declaration such as "whatever principle of intelligence we attain unto in this life, it will rise with us in the resurrection" (D&C 130:18) will be shown to have been prevailing law in connection with the luggage we brought in our coming here from the first estate. How simple. How obvious. How just!

Whether in this life or in the spirit world, those who stood apart from the living God, the living prophets, the living Church, and the living scriptures—will be judged as not having really lived, because those mortals did not understand things as they really are while in mortality. But even they will adjudge God to be merciful and generous.

Those who reveled in their unorthodoxy will be exposed as having left the safety of the stronghold of the saints out of pique and pride, not principle. Other souls who spun off will be exposed as having attempted to elevate one correct principle over all the others, having thereby abused the very principle they said they loved.

All will see that, in reality, *how* we lived, not *how long*, is what matters.

The chronically selfish will learn too late that "a candle is not lighted for itself; neither is a man." (George MacDonald, *Life Essential*, p. 79.)

Those who were drained by difficulties encountered by reason of their righteousness (or whose souls were sorely stretched in service) will find that such experiences have only made room for more understanding and service; all of us will see that conduct created in us increased capacity that, in turn, brought eternal advantage.

Likewise all of us will see how *doing* is linked with *knowing*, and also how *understanding* is irrevocably tied to *obeying*. Those who gave away their sins simply made room to know God. (Alma 22:18.) Those who kept the commandments were actually able to know whether the commandments were of God or man.

Those who shouldered the cross and kept moving will have found that the burden was light and, besides, they will obtain rest from the terrible weariness of the world.

Those who denied themselves will see that righteous living was a great blessing, not a sacrifice, for "Why should a man meditate with satisfaction on having denied himself some selfish indulgence, any more than on having washed his hands?" (George MacDonald, *Life Essential*, p. 86.)

Those who were able in life to give place for gospel things will have, thereby, found a place in the next world that will provide for them even more opportunities for service; while those who were shrunken by selfishness in this life, jettisoning inconvenient babies and aging parents, will have a chance, perhaps firsthand, to face those who were so dispatched or disregarded. Those whose lives were basically a prolonged and profound contraction or a spasm of selfishness will, indeed, wish "the rocks and the mountains to fall" upon them. (Alma 12:14; Revelation 6:16.)

Each of us will find that what we made from the ore of our experience is character, and that character, unlike so many other earthly things acquired, is portable. We will all openly agree that there were for each of us far more unused opportunities that unpleasant inevitabilities.

We shall acknowledge that, while the approaches to death differed, some easy and quick, others slow and agonizing, death itself was simple—the opening of a door to more life, indeed, life everlasting.

At some point in those dramatic sequences, there will come flooding in upon us a fullness of memory of things as they *really were*—in the first estate before we came to earth. These restored remembrances will add greatly to our accountability and to our joy and our anguish—but finally to our gratitude to God. We will actually remember shouting for joy when the plan of happiness was laid before us, way back then. We will thank God for being unvarying in his commitment to that plan of happiness, for though there were mortal moments when we doubted or would have given up, a Perfect Father urged us on and did what he knew to be best "to bring to pass the immortality and eternal life of man." We will praise him for perfect grit and goodness!

Those who wondered or made light of the question of how an obscure religion—just one of many—could be true, will learn that the way to salvation and exaltation is the same on other peopled planets; it is a gospel for the galaxies.

Those who milled about in the valley of decision will see that their touted open-mindedness was merely part of the dynamics of their doubts, and their doubts fed their pride.

We will all see how many times the little chores we did brought large and happy consequences. Those who refused to wait for extraordinary assignments before pursuing the second great commandment will have had the joy of seemingly ordinary chores that, when we see things as they really are, will prove not to have been very ordinary at all. We will also see that to have held oneself in reserve would have been to have missed the fray altogether. Those who deserted their posts in the heat of battle will be asked to face the consequences of what they did—along with Uriah's comrades at arms.

We will all see how the dimension of time was not our natural dimension; hence in mortality we were always so conscious of time, especially as we were caught up in societies that frustrated "our longing at every turn." As Sheldon Vanauken wrote so well, no wonder "we cannot love time. It spoils our loveliest moments." (A Severe Mercy, p. 202.)

We will find with regard to our unrepented-of sins that there will be a "perfect remembrance" and a "bright recollection" of our guilt. Total recall! No wonder some will not wish to lift up their eyes to even glance at God.

We shall all see, and ever so clearly, how Lucifer, an

angel of God, fell from heaven and being "miserable forever, he sought also the misery of all mankind." (2 Nephi 2:18.)

Some will recall humble moments when they stood outside holy things, feeling left out and wondering. But pride soon moved them from hesitant wondering to doubt, and then on to rejection and resentment. It is difficult to admit our ignorance of many things, but it is especially difficult to admit that we have dumbly excluded ourselves from something special. Nevertheless, on that day of judgment, many will say what it is hard to say: that they are self-alienated from God, that they could have been inside holy things. Some will see then that if those multitudes in that spacious building seen by Lehi were so content, why did they spend their time pointing fingers of scorn at the believer? Why was there so much interest within their disinterest?

When these tormented souls, the light of Christ still flickering within them, see things as they really are and as they really will be, they will know for themselves what might have been but that now will never be! Is endless misery too strong a term for such a state? Is "everlasting shame" too express to describe the individual's lost opportunities?

Yet there is a second burden that goes with sin, a deeper dimension of sadness to all of this: the damage our failures and sins do to others. Well might such conclude, "I am here because of me, but he is also here partly because of me!" There is no way to bear such causality with dignity.

Abinadi wrote of this culminating event that will be marked by total concurrence: "The time shall come when all shall see the salvation of the Lord; when every nation, kindred, tongue, and people shall see eye to eye and shall confess before God that his judgments are just." (Mosiah 16:1.) The same thing was foreseen by Isaiah: "Thy watchmen shall lift up the voice; with the voice together shall they sing: for they shall see eye to eye, when the Lord shall bring again Zion." (Isaiah

52:8.)The Savior himself confirmed these prophecies during his visits with the Nephites upon the western hemisphere: "Then shall their watchmen lift up their voice, and with the voice together shall they sing; for they shall see eye to eye." (3 Nephi 20:32.)

These great and glorious things will be, "For since the beginning of the world have not men heard nor perceived by the ear, neither hath any eye seen, O God, besides thee, how great things thou hast prepared for him that waiteth for thee. And it shall be said: Who is this that cometh down from God in heaven with dyed garments; yea, from the regions which are not known, clothed in his glorious apparel, traveling in the greatness of his strength? And he shall say: I am he who spake in righteousness, mighty to save. And the Lord shall be red in his apparel, and his garments like him that treadeth in the wine-vat. And so great shall be the glory of his presence that the sun shall hide his face in shame, and the moon shall withhold its light, and the stars shall be hurled from their places." (D&C 133: 45-49.)

This glorious time of blessings, as well as judgment, was also described in the words of the ancient prophet Isaiah: "For since the beginning of the world men have not heard, nor perceived by the ear, neither hath the eye seen, O God, beside thee, what he hath prepared for him that waiteth for him." (Isaiah 64:4.)

The words of the apostle Paul are parallel: ". . . it is written, Eye hath not seen, nor ear heard, neither have entered into the heart of man, the things which God hath prepared for them that love him." (1 Corinthians 2:9.)

The best mortal music we have heard will be surpassed by the sounds of celestial chords we shall hear there. The most beautiful art and scenery experienced in the here and now of this earth will have scarcely prepared us for the beauties we shall see then and there.

The pain of the judgment will be followed by the overwhelming blessings the living and loving Father has prepared for us. Those who hear the words "Well done, thou good and faithful servant, . . . enter thou into the joy of thy lord" (Matthew 25:21), will be filled with unspeakable joy. Those so adjudged can say of their own tiny trek, "It is finished," and yet so much will have just begun!

We will be home, and the promise to us is that God will land our souls, yea, our immortal souls, "at the right hand of God in the kingdom of heaven, to sit down with Abraham, and Isaac, and with Jacob, and with all our holy fathers, to go no more out." (Helaman 3:30.) Never again will we be really away from Him!

Those who in this life have "let the solemnities of eternity" rest upon them (D&C 43:34), and who have acted on the basis of "things as they really will be," can appreciate that what we will enjoy then was planned long, long ago: "According to that which was ordained in the midst of the Council of the Eternal God of all other gods before this world was, that should be reserved unto the finishing and the end thereof, when every man shall enter into his eternal presence and into his immortal rest." (D&C 121:32.)

If we live correctly now, we need not hide our eyes then, for we can, with Enos, "see his face with pleasure, and he will say unto [us], Come unto me, ye blessed, there is a place prepared for you in the mansions of my Father." (Enos 1:27.)

"Reality," how things really are, and "verity," the true way to respond to reality, and "felicity," the joy and happiness that are realizable—these are beneficially blended only in the gospel of Jesus Christ. It's no use being grieved with God, as some are, because mortality is not a multiple-choice situation; there is a solitary system for human happiness now and an exclusive route to happiness in the world to come. Pouting, even sophisticated pouting, will not change reality. It does no good, either, to withhold oneself from the fray wishing things were otherwise, for pride piles upon pride, weighing us down and lessening our mobility. Trails are made for mobile climbers, including the straight and narrow way.

Each soul must—now or later—surrender to God. At that moment the universe becomes a vast home, rather than a majestic but hostile maze. Surprisingly with such surrender comes victory, and never have any received such surrender terms. To yield to him is to receive *all* that he has!

SOURCES CITED

Bartlett, John. *Bartlett's Familiar Quotations.* London: Macmillan and Co., 1968 ed.

Journal of Discourses. Brigham Young and others. 26 vols. Liverpool: F.D. and S.W. Richards, 1854-86.

Lewis, C. S. *A Mind Awake.* New York: Harcourt, Brace & World, 1968.

MacDonald, George. *An Anthology.* London: Geoffrey Bles, 1970.

——————. *Life Essential.* Wheaton, Illinois: Harold Shaw Publishers, 1974.

Smith, Joseph. *History of The Church of Jesus Christ of Latter-day Saints.* 7 vols. Salt Lake City: Deseret Book, 1950. (Volume 7 is a manuscript history of Brigham Young.)

Smith, Joseph F. *Gospel Doctrine.* Compiled by Joseph Fielding Smith. Salt Lake City: Deseret Book, 1939.

Smith, Joseph Fielding. *Doctrines of Salvation.* 3 vols. Salt Lake City: Bookcraft, 1954-56.

Talmage, James E. *The Great Apostasy.* Salt Lake City: Deseret Book, 1975.

Taylor, John. *The Gospel Kingdom.* Salt Lake City: Bookcraft, 1943.

Trimble, John R. *Writing with Style.* Englewood Cliffs, New Jersey: Prentice-Hall, 1975.

Will, George F. *The Pursuit of Happiness and Other Sobering Thoughts.* New York: Harper & Row, 1978.

INDEX

29; followed his Father's
example in all things, 22-23;
sheep of, recognize him, 25,
104-5; asked about nine
lepers, 56; foresaw growth
of Church, 59; second
coming of, 118
John the Baptist, 108-9
John the Revelator, 111-12
Jonah, 36
Joseph in Egypt, 55-56
Joy, xiv
Judgment day, 92-93, 111-19

Kimball, Spencer W.: on
prophets, 65, 68-69; on
revelation, 69
Kingdom: Church is, 45; to fill
whole earth, 46
Knowledge: of things as they
really are, value of, 3, 4;
growth of faith into, 10; is
tied to behavior, 49, 58
Korihor, 7-8, 62

Lamanites, conversion of, 96-97
Language, complexity of, 54-55,
107-8
Larsen, Dean L., on sons of
Mosiah, 96-97
Last days, prophecies
concerning, 94
Learning, 95
Lee, Harold B., 70-71
Lehi, 13
Lewis, C. S.: on perspective, 10;
on measuring, 48; on
priorities, 61; on associating
with evil, 86
Liberty, 2
Life has ultimate meaning, 16
Light: of gospel, breaking forth
of, 63-64; children of, 93
"Living," connotation of, 46
Loneliness, 6

Love: unfeigned, 89; waxing
cold of, 94
Lucifer, xiii

MacDonald, George: on being
at home with the Lord, 17;
on trusting God, 54; on
necessity of shock, 66
Memory, restoration of, at
judgment, 115
Moral decline, consequences of,
20
Mormon, 29
Mosiah, sons of, 96-97
Mother, Heavenly, 67
Moyle, Henry D., 31

Net, gospel, xiii
Neutral, none will stand, 60
Noah, corruption at time of, 76

"O My Father," 67
Omniscience of God, 22
Oracles, living, 67-68
Ordinances, 51
Outer space, 5, 21

Packer, Boyd K., 47
"Past feeling," wicked described
as being, 88-89
Patience, 88
Paul: teachings of, on
foreordination, 23;
preached against idolatry,
66; on thorn in flesh, 91; on
simplicity, 104
Persecution, fear of, 91
Perspective: loss of, 6-7, 21, 54;
of reality, 10
Peter, 77
Piano keyboard, Church likened
to, 47
Plainness, 105-6
Politics, Church involvement in,
60-61